MILITARY WIFE FIELD MANUAL

FINDING YOUR PLACE IN HIS WORLD

Heather Eberhart

This is a work of nonfiction. However, certain names and identifying details have been changed to protect the privacy of those involved.

Copyright © 2022 by Heather Eberhart

All rights reserved. No part of this book may be reproduced or used in any manner without written permission of the copyright owner except for the use of quotations in a book review. For more information, address:
heather@heathereberhart.com

ISBN: 979-8-9869726-1-9

Scripture quotations marked NLT are taken from the *Holy Bible*, New Living Translation, copyright © 1996, 2004, 2015 by Tyndale House Foundation. Used by permission of Tyndale House Publishers, Inc., Carol Stream, Illinois 60188. All rights reserved.

Scripture quotations marked NIV are taken from The Holy Bible, New International Version® NIV® copyright © 1973, 1978, 1984, 2011 by Biblica, Inc.™ Used by permission. All rights reserved worldwide.

First Printing, 2022

Cover design: Andrea Flores

Internal design: Chrissy Wolfe, EFC Services, LLC

Headshot: Tonya Tillman

heathereberhart.com

CONTENTS

- CHAPTER 1 - NOT AN ETIQUETTE GUIDE _____ 1

- CHAPTER 2 - BELIEF IN THE MISSION _____ 11

  The Marriage Model; It's a Lifestyle; Not Hearing, But Listening; What Does Your Husband Do?; Expectations? No Thank You; Kill Resentment; Know the Roles; Decision-Making; Words Matter; Belief in the Mission: Review

- CHAPTER 3 - RIGHT VS. WRONG COMMUNITY _____ 51

  Support System; Characteristics of the Right Community; Red Flags; Do I Belong?; Finding Friends; Spill the Tea; Setting Boundaries; Battling Loneliness; Made for Right Now; Right vs. Wrong Community: Review

- CHAPTER 4 - IDENTITY MATTERS _____ 88

  Time to Mourn; Proverbs Model; Wellness Routines; Morning Routines; Evening Routines; Sleep Struggle; Daily Affirmations; Stay Committed; Identity Matters: Review

- CHAPTER 5 - VALUE OF MENTORSHIP _____ 125

  Needing Guidance; Train the Young; Made for Encouragement; Be Invitational; A Good Mentor Listens; Confident Leadership; Open for Accountability; Trust One Another; Compassionate Hearts; Use What You Have; Value of Mentorship: Review

- CHAPTER 6 - PURPOSED FOR MILITARY WIFE LIFE _____ 160

When Reality Sucks; Personal Dreams and Vision; Ready to Quit; Living with Hope; Through the Lens of Love; Stay Grateful; Repeat After Me: Mantras; Replacing Lies with Truth; Jacked Priorities; Purposed for Military Wife Life: Review

- CHAPTER 7 - BE WHO YOU ARE _____ 194

- ACKNOWLEDGMENTS -

- SUGGESTED READING -

- ABOUT THE AUTHOR -

- REFERENCES -

– CHAPTER 1 –
NOT AN ETIQUETTE GUIDE

There I was, sitting on a blanket on an unfamiliar base with four crying children in my lap. I was shedding more internal tears than they could have ever wept aloud. It was a sunny Saturday during the summer and the kids' first trip to the aquarium at our new duty station. We had just moved from Mississippi to Virginia after two years of back-to-back deployments. My husband and I were excited to be together again after so much separation, and the kids loved that Dad was home again and were ecstatic about having a day together — a day without unpacking boxes. If there was ever such a thing as a perfect day, this was going to be it.

The morning was packed with stingrays, sharks, sea turtles, and what felt like millions of smiles. Halfway through our explorations a lunch break was needed. We found an eating area outside and sat down at a picnic table overlooking the creek. I had barely finished opening chip bags, cutting chicken tenders, and popping straws into juice boxes before a phone rang. I could barely breathe as I looked at my husband. I managed to ask, "That's your work phone, isn't it?" With a resigned look, one I'd seen dozens of times in our military tenure, he walked to a quiet corner of the picnic area and answered the call.

It's what they're trained to do - answer the call.

We, as military wives, know this. We live this reality every single day, but how we handle these moments varies with each passing season. On this particular Saturday afternoon, I felt angry. I felt tricked. This was supposed to be our perfect day after two long years of sacrifice and separation. This was supposed to be an uninterrupted family day. I watched as he paced around the picnic area, still on the phone. My insides were crawling with worst case scenarios, but I kept my cool in front of the kids. Even when the military sends us to new places or calls our husbands away, military wives know how to be strong on the outside, whether it's for our kids or for our husbands. It isn't always as easy to keep it together on the inside. I had a decision to make that day. Would I control my emotions and deal with this difficult situation? Or would I let my inner two-year-old shine through and throw a temper tantrum about his work always interrupting?

For five minutes I watched him pace. I circled the table, continuing to help our four kids eat their lunches, unable to sit because of how nervous I felt. I kept trying to make eye contact with him from across the picnic area, watching his facial expressions, desperate to know if the military was calling him away from us again. Finally, he put his phone back in his pocket. We locked eyes, and I knew our time at the aquarium was over. The Navy needed him. Before I could process this sudden new reality, we were packing up the remains of our lunch, buckling tearful children into the car, and silently driving the thirty minutes to base. Our hopeful, perfect day was over whether we were ready or not. Our man had a duty to carry out, and I would stand beside him no matter what. On the inside I wanted to kick and scream. On the inside I wanted to throw passive-aggressive explanations at my kids, telling them how it was Dad's fault we had to leave the aquarium early. On the inside I wanted to tell him it wasn't fair; this new duty station was supposed to be a break for him and give our family a normal schedule. He wasn't supposed to deal with interruptions.

Because of whatever was said during that phone call, there was no time to take us home, so Mike dropped me and the kids at a park while he drove several blocks over to his office. The park swings and slide were a poor replacement for penguins and seahorses, but I squeezed every lemon I could find that day to make the most of the situation. I tried my hardest to silence the negative comment reel racing through my mind, but I must admit, in those moments I was thinking what to say to my husband and with how much attitude, how unfair the whole situation was, and how long I could hold it against him. Even though my mind was full of negativity, I made sure to put on a brave face for the kids. My outside was kept in check, but the internal battle was far from perfect.

The five of us spent several hours at the park. We finished our lunches on a blanket and prayed for Dad through tears and sniffles. We played tag and waited to see what would happen next. Was this something his command could handle remotely? Would he have to pack his bags and leave? What was happening and how long would it be before I knew our next steps? But most of all I kept asking myself, is he really going to leave me alone with these kids again? I needed help after two years of deployments. I had my own dreams and visions I wanted to pursue. It was supposed to be my turn!

Just when I began to think I couldn't keep the kids occupied much longer, Mike's picture lit up my cell phone. He was done with work and the situation was resolved without any further action. We were able to return home that evening as a family of six, safe and sound, still intact.

That Saturday continues to be a reminder for me to stay humble. The life of a military wife is unpredictable and challenging. The narrative we play in our minds majorly impacts how we handle the challenges.

The turmoil we battle within our minds between our sacrificial lifestyle and the desire for our own pursuits is worse when we don't understand where we belong. When we cannot confidently find our place in his world, it's hard to shift our mindset to what matters most. It's hard to see military wife life clearly when we feel like we don't have a place. It's hard to know how to be a great wife, mother, friend, and woman, when we struggle to belong in his military world. This becomes apparent when we find ourselves in a situation like my aquarium story. The narrative playing in my mind didn't match who I was on the outside, because I was searching for my place as a military wife.

I'm a Navy wife of over thirteen years and the tension I feel between supporting my husband in his service to this country and my own heart's desires still feels overwhelming some days. A military wife's job is unique and challenging and heart-wrenching and joyous and all of the things. We sometimes feel like we are living everyone else's life but our own. We keep all the plates spinning during deployments. We walk on eggshells during reintegration.

We smile in the sun during leave. We are here for the highs and the lows. We have a hard job.

Even after thirteen years of marriage in the military, I still feel like I am learning something brand new daily. The acronyms are plentiful and the uncertainty is certain. But there are a handful of things I have been able to carry with me; things I believe if I would have known from the beginning, our military experience so far could have been much improved. Through the newlywed period, the years we spent having and raising babies, deployment cycles, and now, I can look back with some assurance and say I believe there is a process to this lifestyle. I can comb through my experiences and those of my fellow military wives to find core values of being a strong military wife. Sure, it looks different for everyone, but there are a few key things we can do as military wives to help serve our husbands while still finding our place. In this book we'll walk through it all and you'll learn more about discovering who you are and where you fit in his world. You'll put in the hard work because you are created to be here and have something powerful to share.

That's what this is, his world. For most of us the military life wasn't the original plan. You may have had dreams and visions of your own before your husband came along. Sure, you willingly and excitedly married him whether you knew what was ahead of you or not. But the day you entered into this covenant, not only with God and your husband but with this country, you accepted a responsibility — to serve this great nation by serving him. There are parts of the military journey which ring true for every wife wanting more from her husband's military career. There is a path, a system of beliefs, building blocks. A woman desperate to find her place and purpose beside her husband will need these steps.

This Field Manual will walk you through a five-part process to move from resentment and despair to hope and freedom so you can stand firm in your place as a military wife. Think of it as building blocks for a strong military wife life.

If you have ever wondered how you are going to make it through the day, this book is for you. If you have ever wondered when it is going to be your turn, this book is for you. If you have ever wondered how you're going to manage to make friends each and every time you move, this book is for you. If you have wondered how you will find your identity outside of military life, how you will continue to fight for your marriage when your husband is hardly ever home, how you're going to keep your mental health in check when you have no control over what's next, this book is for you.

The Military Wife Field Manual is not necessarily a linear list of to-dos, but building blocks to living military wife life well. The soul work needed to find your place isn't an overnight change. I will provide you with tools along the way, but the real work begins with your mindset. We start with foundation work as you begin to believe in the mission. A dear friend of mine and fellow Navy wife Monica says it like this, "You have to drink the Kool-Aid and be ALL IN!" Correcting and adjusting your mindset toward your military marriage lays the groundwork for finding your place. We'll spend time learning why it's important for you to understand your husband's role, the military as a whole, and the path the Lord has set before you as a family. This takes time, patience, persistence, and understanding. Throughout this phase, you must be diligent about having hard conversations because this is the only way you will truly believe in the mission.

Once you're onboard with your family, you will need to understand the importance of the community around you. The right community is invaluable and surrounding yourself with encouraging women will help guide you in a healthy direction. Strong friendships will also help keep you accountable to embrace the mission. Community is a necessary next step as you learn where you belong as a military wife. You will start to see the importance of life-giving military spouse groups, church, and Bible studies.

The third belief and building block on your path is a giant step, and one many military wives struggle with. You must believe you are essential: the right woman for the job. Your value and worth do not come from how well you survive deployment, but from the Lord. You will learn the value of self-care because your service member needs to know you are fully healthy and capable of holding down the household when he is away. You are the most valuable piece in this puzzle and your confidence will help your husband focus on his calling. You are made for this and so much more. Once you have a solid foundation within your marriage and a healthy community surrounding you for support, caring for yourself and diving into your true identity becomes easier. Trying to do the inner work first is hard when you are alone. It's during this step when we lean into your dreams outside of military wife life. The real work of finding your place in each season happens here.

To add to your sense of worth and because it's necessary for the overall health of our military spouse community, the fourth step is about helping others. By this time, you have three building blocks of experience to pull from. You can become an invaluable resource to other wives. You can learn to mentor and serve.

The final step is being able to carry on with hope. Without courage and hope, your building blocks may crumble over time. You may find yourself on roads of brokenness and struggle. Military wife life can be amazing even when it looks different than what you imagined, but you must have hope. Fully believing you are purposed for military wife life is your final declaration as you stand in your place.

The Military Wife Field Manual Building Blocks

- I believe in the mission.
- I believe the right community is invaluable.
- I believe I am essential.
- I am a resource to other military wives.
- I am purposed for military wife life.

This isn't your average how-to handbook. This is not the 1925 Etiquette Guide that says if the Army wanted him to have a wife, they would have issued one. You aren't simply learning to survive your time here. You are purposed for more. Throughout the book, you'll also see stories of other military wives. Like I said before, each wife's journey is unique, but we carry the same building blocks as we pursue living military life with purpose. These sections are called "Battle Buddies" because our greatest weapon against the negative narratives we play in our minds is our community. Be inspired by the stories these women share and take their lessons with you as you find your place. Living military wife life from the sidelines isn't an option anymore. The images of long-ago military wives pining for their husbands during deployments and keeping a perfect home as housewives are in the past. We are a new generation of wives with a higher calling. Is it scary? Yes. Does reading this cause feelings of fear, frustration, guilt, pride, anxiousness, or worry to course through our veins? Yes. Will we let any of those keep us from thriving in our calling? Absolutely not.

Military wife, we can be the helpers we are created to be. We can do it on the easy days, the impossible days, the lonely days, the uncertain days, and every day in between. Know these things as we dive in. You are seen. The desires of your heart are still valid. Your story is still being written. Whether you feel like you have a clear path ahead of you or you feel like you're spinning, lost and alone, take comfort in knowing there is a journey planned for you. I'll share my story with you because that's what I am purposed to do. It's *my place* in his world. I'll share with you how I learned to support the mission of the military as a unified family and started looking to the Lord to lead our journey. I'll share the things most uncomfortable to share because I am and have been where you are. I want nothing more than to help guide you to a place of peace and contentedness as you stand in *your place*.

You have a place in his world. You don't have to sacrifice who you are to support him. In reality, he needs the best version of you in order for him to do his job well. Let's learn how you can make it happen.

– CHAPTER 2 –
BELIEF IN THE MISSION

"While your husband's military assignments are clearly spelled out in his transfer orders, your assignment can be found in a different document: your marriage certificate."
– Jocelyn Green, Faith Deployed

The Marriage Model 16
It's a Lifestyle 18
Not Hearing, But Listening 21
What Does Your Husband Do? 25
Expectations? No Thank You 29
Kill Resentment 34
Know the Roles 38
Decision-Making 41
Words Matter 44
Belief in the Mission: Review 49

It was a Sunday morning before church. There was coffee brewing, possibly breakfast cooking, but that detail escapes me. Four tiny children were playing and fussing in the background. In the moment, however, I didn't smell or hear any of it. The love of my life had just entered the kitchen of our rented Mississippi home, stumbling along, coming out of sleep. And hungover.

The tears came slow at first. I stood in front of the sink, trying not to make eye contact. I had held it in for too long, though. When he quietly announced he didn't feel like going to church, I snapped like an overtightened guitar string. Sobs and shouts and rage came flooding out, all directed toward the man I married half a decade earlier. "WE WERE BETTER OFF WITHOUT YOU! WE DON'T NEED YOU ANYMORE! WHY DON'T YOU JUST LEAVE?" I screamed until my vocal cords ached. My husband had never been a big drinker, but post-deployment freedoms were catching up to him. Living with a bunch of dudes for several months had changed his habits. It didn't help that he came home to a well-established routine of everything revolving around three babies and a toddler. I didn't allow him to enter back into our lives, and I can guess he didn't really know where he fit anymore. I was unfamiliar. His kids were strangers. His home was overrun with toys, bottles, dirty diapers, burp cloths, and mounds of laundry in various stages of cleanliness. I didn't allow him space. After all, I ran this household solo for several months, and I selfishly wanted him to be proud we were all still alive and well. No wonder he needed a few beers!

I had lived for months on end having to do it all alone. He had lived for months on end working around the clock. After the kids went to bed each night, I watched reality TV shows. He put his headphones on and watched war movies. I hosted coffee chats and went to a book club once a month. He toured cities and went scuba diving. I got hugs and kisses from our four beautiful children every single day. No one touched him for months. Our worlds were vastly different. Working to incorporate each other back into our lives was work — awkward, heart-wrenching work. Simple things like letting him take the trash out on garbage day was easy! But watching him figure out how to discipline our children again? No one tells you how to do this. Navigating re-entry is no easy task and tears will always be shed. It's one of the hardest parts of military wife life.

The first few days, even weeks, after a homecoming are bliss. He's home! You go back to dating each other. You're on your best behavior and possibly even on high alert because you're still getting to know this semi-unfamiliar person again. The military likes to call this period "reintegration". Most commands will hand out a packet assuring families of the normalcy of reintegration frustrations. They give you checklists and graphs thinking they will help because slideshows and PDFs are all they know. In one sentence they tell him to re-enter slowly, and in the next tell him to spend maximum time with family. Cue the confusion. No matter which way you spin it, reintegration is an arduous journey. There is no formula other than realizing that at some point the ball will drop. Things will come crashing down and nothing will feel easy or comfortable anymore.

The reintegration process for that particular deployment was extremely difficult and the moments of frustration continued to build, right up until I told him to leave. Let it be known that this is *my* account of the story and how *I* processed the situation. My husband certainly saw the whole thing from another angle. To me, this day was monumental in our story, but to him it may have just been a speed bump. Keeping perspective is key when looking back on these moments. I can say that now.

So there we were, me sobbing and him hungover. We had silently danced around each other for weeks, but the storm had arrived. As I continued screaming, he was inching his way closer. I wanted him to leave, and he wanted to close the gap. For a thousand and one reasons this behavior made me want to punch him even more. When I am mad, I want to stay mad and sit in those feelings. I think I will enjoy the self-sabotage. I secretly want everyone to notice things aren't going my way. This is not my husband. He is a fixer. He wants things to be remedied as quickly as possible. He doesn't storm off in a rage, he calmly diffuses situations and brings peace. Lord, have mercy, I can't stand this some days. Especially when I am trying to control a situation that feels very out of control — like him not meeting my post-deployment expectations. Our family life was a downright mess and a half, and he wants to hug it out? Watch out. I shuffled and dodged my way around the kitchen, ignoring crying babies and morning cartoons. He walked along trying to corner me so he could bring me into his embrace. Eventually, he won. Feeling as if I couldn't cry any more tears, I stood rigid in his arms. Nope, I absolutely would not hug him back (you showed him, Heather). He is a man of few words, but he said he was sorry and would work on it. Did we go to church? I have no idea. In my heart I want to be able to say yes, but I don't remember.

The argument was never about church. It was a whole lot of things, but attending church wasn't one of them. I can look back now and see how broken we both were. I thought I had everything together and he was the only messed up one. Lord only knows what Mike saw when he came home from deployment. I can see now I had a lot of feelings I was unable to process while he was gone. I felt lonely, unqualified, sad, unworthy, angry, jealous, fearful, and most of all I felt like I was living without purpose. All of those emotions spewed out into the world when he was still feeling confused about where he fit in.

We all have stories like this. It's just part of military life, right? Yes and no. The uncertainty, yes. The deployments, yes. The reintegration, yes. We don't get to ditch those, but we can embrace how we view them. Again, keeping perspective is key. But what we learned the day I told him to leave was this; there was a disconnect between his job, our marriage, and our family. We didn't fully believe in the mission. And without being able to fully embrace his job as our lifestyle, it was near impossible for me to find my place.

I call this section the foundation block because the health of your marriage dictates how well you will be able to navigate your place as a military wife. I screamed across the kitchen at my husband that day because we weren't fully committed to living military life together. I viewed my place outside his role as a service member, and our marriage, our family, suffered. We obviously didn't end our marriage that morning, but it taught us just how strong our foundation needed to be to live military life well. It opened my eyes to how much I needed to live military wife life with a posture of acceptance instead of always fighting against it.

Throughout this chapter you will learn how to navigate being married to a military man, discussing expectations, roles, resentment, and decision-making. We do this not because it is what we *should* do, but because it is what *must* be done in order to build a strong enough foundation to stand on as you pursue your place in his world.

THE MARRIAGE MODEL

When you stood before your husband on your wedding day, you promised each other many things. You vowed to be his person on the easy days and in the hard seasons. Your marriage certificate carries weight, but even before that covenant was made, the model for marriage was formed in the image of Creation. From the beginning of time, man was made to answer the call. The very first book of the Bible gives us the framework, saying, "Then the Lord God formed the man from the dust of the ground. He breathed the breath of life into the man's nostrils, and the man became a living person.[1] "It goes on to say, "The Lord God placed the man in the Garden of Eden to tend and watch over it."[2]

Man was created from the dust of the Earth and placed here to fill a specific purpose, to answer the call. This worked well for a little while before God said, "It is not good for the man to be alone. I will make a helper who is just right for him."[3] God then created a woman from the man's own body. She was created to be his helper. Our God is a purposeful God, and nothing He does is random or accidental. There is a reason He created man first, assigned him a job second, and created him a helper third. Adam's first duty was to answer the call: to fulfill the job the Lord gave him. Eve's place was beside Adam as his

---

[1] Genesis 2:7 NLT
[2] Genesis 2:15 NLT
[3] Genesis 2:18 NLT

helper. The Lord knew that for Adam to do his job well, he would need someone by his side. Your husband is called to serve this nation and you, as his wife, are created to be his helper.

You may be reading this thinking, *Gosh, Heather, you are crazy. I am a strong woman who wants a career. We are simply making this military life work until he can get out.* Our culture today loves to tell women they need independence, a career, and strength. Singleness, just like married life, is a calling and perfect for some, but this is the Military WIFE Field Manual. Your thoughts of *making it work* are valid and there is nothing wrong with them, but you don't have to settle. You're allowed to want more. You're allowed to want to find a sense of purpose somewhere in the jumble of deployments and dishes. In order to find your place though, you must have a solid foundation, and that starts within your military marriage regardless of what culture deems necessary or important.

A practical example of keeping this model in mind during everyday life is when you are looking for a way to fill your days at each new duty station. If you begin job hunting or looking for volunteer opportunities, ask yourself how it will impact your role as a wife to your husband. Ask yourself if all the needs of the family can be met while also adding in something else. Ask yourself if there are issues within your marriage that may need attention before accepting a position outside the home. Saying yes to one thing means saying no to something else, but if you say no to the foundation while saying yes to the roof, you'll never end up with a secure structure.

Hear me when I say, you can confidently stand in your

calling while pursuing a career. You can serve your husband well while finding your place in his world, but if you struggle to accept the order of the Creation story, you will find this journey very difficult. The Lord hand-picked your husband to serve this nation. It's no easy calling. Your husband is fulfilling a very specific purpose. He has a responsibility to uphold, and the truth is, he can't do it alone. He needs a helper. Just as the Lord created him to work, you are created to help. The Lord created and hand-picked you to help your husband in his calling. This is the foundation of finding your place as a military wife. There is room for you to pursue your passions, but when added to a crumbling foundation, your personal life will suffer. When focusing on creating a strong military family foundation, remember the order of creation and reflect it in your marriage.

IT'S A LIFESTYLE

When we were kids my brother had a good friend who became known for one thing. He absolutely could not handle when different foods on his plate were touching. For a long time, we watched this friend eat one thing at a time. He scooped a pile of green beans on his plate, ate every last one, and then and only then could he place the chicken on his plate. Moving from one food to the next became his norm because heaven forbid if those foods touched each other before finding their way to his stomach. Let's not even get started on how he handled gravy. This learned behavior changed when we started keeping divided plates in our home just for him. He could load up his plate while still sectioning off the mashed potatoes from the steak. Hallelujah! This was a perceived victory, but still not an absolute solution. After all, you can't ask for divided plates at restaurants. It took time and maturity, but eventually our friend progressed in the food world. He can now have all his foods on one beautifully open plate.

For five years Mike and I were like this friend. We were lovers of the divided plate. Each piece of our lives had its own place on the plate with walls built up in protection. The messy stickiness of parenting never touched the clean cuts of military life. We compartmentalized because we thought it was easier and cleaner. Sure, it may have looked neater from the outside, but life is never not messy. Building walls to contain the mess was never going to work. Just like our friend, it took a lot of time and maturity, but these days Mike and I embrace one plate. We are lovers of all the foods touching and their flavors mixing. Is it messy? Absolutely! But we've come to understand it's better to be in the mess together than be orderly but separate.

We believe in the mission of this lifestyle. We believe whole-heartedly we are called to be a military family: Mike serving active-duty and his family supporting him. We cannot continue separating his work from our lives. We are either all in or heartbreakingly disconnected. This is where military life and civilian life differ greatly. In the civilian word people have the luxury (or disadvantage, however you want to look at it) of having a job they can easily detach from every day at 5 p.m. There's an off switch on their computer. They can lock their office door and walk away. Military life isn't like this. I wouldn't want to change it, but it does force us to rethink how our plate is organized. Military service members don't simply have a job, they have an entire lifestyle. They live on boats, deploy around the world, carry duty phones, stand watch, and serve this country with pride. It's a way of life, not a job. And how dare we, as their spouses, view their work as anything less. We are their cheerleader, supporter, sounding board, and helper. We have the honor and privilege of staying behind so our service members can serve our nation well.

Mike's first deployment ended in me asking him to leave because my mindset hadn't yet shifted from our sectioned way of living to standing together in the mess. I stomped around day after day feeling resentment toward him because he *got* to go away. He *got* to have adult friends. He *got* to escape the sleepless nights with three newborns at home. Had I been able to shift my perspective, his return home may have been different. This is where we step into murky water. Yes, you are called to stand beside him and support him. You are called to carry the weight alone sometimes. But that doesn't mean it won't suck the ever-loving life from your soul. Military life is *hard*. Change is certain and schedules shift often. Kids will cry their tiny eyes out when Dad gets deployed, and you'll be the one to pick up the pieces. The strength it takes to get through these moments is unmatched.

There will be times when you forget your higher calling, times you will feel unaccustomed to this way of life. You'll have moments when you'll forget this isn't just his job, but a way of life. It's in these moments when you need grace the most. But this is all part of finding your place. At the heart of every military wife's job description are tiny moments of steadfastness and support. When you can accept military life as a lifestyle and the level of commitment involved, it helps you find your place.

NOT HEARING, BUT LISTENING

As you continue to build the strong foundation needed for finding your place as a military wife, you need to lean into some of the issues within your marriage. We've probably all heard how important communication is as married people, but there's one specific conversation that irritates me above all the rest. Maybe it's because it is the same every day when he walks through the door. Or maybe it's because no matter how much it bothers me, it doesn't seem to change. It may be slightly different for you, but in our house, it goes a lot like this:

> *It's the witching hour and my husband comes through the front door after a long day on base. He drops his backpack in the foyer, gently steps around the mess in the living room and says, "Hey babe. How was your day?" as he walks into the kitchen where I am preparing dinner.*
>
> *In my mind I unload the entire day step by step, hour by hour. In my mind I spew every last detail onto his already full brain, how messy that one diaper change was, how much I cleaned or didn't, how frustrating it was to be stuck at home with the kids all day. Instead, I surrender the quiet words, "Oh, pretty good. You?"*
>
> *He knowingly doesn't want to pry any deeper, so he replies, "Yeah, it was good." And that's it. We each silently crave the love and attention of the other, but selfishly can't ask the harder questions. It leaves us feeling disconnected,*

unseen, and unloved.

If I'm honest, there are days when I don't want anything more than this exact conversation. If I'm standing at the kitchen counter simultaneously cooking dinner and helping our third grader with homework, I don't want to know how his meeting went. I don't want him to tell me he went out for lunch with his buddies. I don't want to hear how his day was full of purpose. A small part of me wants him to feel my struggle — like what I do in this life doesn't matter. There are days I am too insecure to hear more than "good" when I ask about his day. But other days I want to feel seen, heard, and validated. I want him to reassure me that I am purposed for this life. And I want to be that person for him, too. I crave the details of a day he perceives to be boring. I want to be his cheerleader. You're allowed to feel each end of this range of emotions. But in order to push through and make progress in marital communication, you must believe that what he does is important, and vice versa. It's a lifestyle you live together on an open plate, so your messes are allowed to touch. You need to be ready to have open, respectful conversation, but also listen and engage. You have to be ready to hear the details even if you feel insecure. And most importantly, you have to be willing to ask more questions on the days he isn't willing to share.

If you feel all kinds of squirmy, you're in good company. This is hard, selfless work. When stories beginning with acronyms fill the space between dinner sizzling and kids playing, it's easy to check out. If you've heard it once, you've heard it a hundred times, but allow me to bring some truth. "Be quick to listen, slow to speak, and slow to get angry."[4] It is simple advice but it comes with a cost. Living this way, being "quick to listen," means you have to break down small pieces of your own walls. Living this way means you have to fight through your feelings of unworthiness. You have to declare that you are invested in this life because you believe in the mission. Craving your place in his military world and being quick to listen is one more tool you can use to solidify your foundation.

A good listener has no ulterior motive, no selfish agenda. You must do the hard work and have the hard conversations because at the end of the day you love your husband, want a strong foundation, and want more from this military life as you find your place. Unity in marriage through listening will create a stronger, more honest relationship. Sometimes this means planning for more purposeful conversations. I know when Mike and I need to work on our budget or talk about his next set of orders, we set aside time on the calendar. This is especially true if you have younger kids running around — it can be hard to have an uninterrupted conversation. Send the kids outside for ten minutes so the two of you can talk with each other sans distractions. Something I like to try to make happen is to sneak outside and meet Mike in the driveway when he gets home from work. Any way to make those important conversations between you and your husband happen is worth the effort. It helps the two of you stay grounded and of one mind.

I am always working toward being a better listener. I'm

---

[4] James 1:19 NLT

not naturally good at listening and retaining information. One way I try to be better is by making eye contact. I know it sounds simple, but all too often I find myself listening to my husband as I am scrolling on my phone. I get irritated when other people do this to me, so why is it any different within my marriage? Good eye contact from the listener makes the speaker feel seen and heard.

I know I am also guilty of not letting him speak complete thoughts. I need to practice waiting my turn to speak. We teach our kids this — to wait patiently to speak if we are talking with another adult — but I don't always follow the same advice. It's quite hard to listen well if we aren't quiet! As women, I think we often believe we know a better or different way to approach a situation or have something of value to add to the conversation, but listening isn't always about winning or even being helpful. Some conversations just need to be about letting someone vent or process. Another tool I sometimes use when I am trying to be a better listener is physical touching while talking. It's a powerful tool and one I don't always think about. Try holding you husband's hand (if you don't have a baby hanging off of you and a toddler at your feet) or placing your hand on his arm. This helps hold each other's attention as you listen and communicate.

Is it realistic to do all these things every day he walks through the front door? Absolutely not. But if I am in a tough season and communication feels difficult, I keep these tools in mind to help ease our conversations.

As you learn to be a better listener within your marriage, it's important to ask questions. There will be plenty of things you don't understand throughout the conversations you'll have as a military wife. Ask him what you don't know. Engage with him and extract details about his day. For some, listening comes easy. For others like me, it's something to work at constantly. Remember, listening is a way to show love. Love your husband well by listening and caring enough to ask questions along the way. As you hone your listening and conversation skills, the foundation of your marriage will strengthen.

WHAT DOES YOUR HUSBAND DO?

Have you ever been caught in a moment with a blank look on your face when someone asks you, "What does your husband do in the military?" I have! You can brush it off easily thinking it's too hard to explain, but do you really know what he does? The importance of understanding his work, his world, cannot be understated. It may seem like a trivial thing, maybe even one you think you can skip over or rush through, but don't be fooled. This simple yet difficult practice can help lay a solid foundation for the rest of your time in the military, a solid foundation for your marriage. You must commit to learn, understand, and care about what your husband does and how it impacts your entire family. Yes, there is a lot to learn about the military and the branch your husband is serving in. It's hard work to create enough brain space for acronyms to live. You don't have to be perfect, but you do need an answer when someone asks you what your husband does for a living. This not only helps him feel supported and validated, but it can lessen your moments of frustration.

We talked about listening being an important aspect of the foundation of your marriage, and we must now also introduce the impact learning can have. Listening to your husband as he goes through his day is one part, but what happens when you engage and ask questions? What if he answers with things you don't understand? You must commit to learn. The combination of listening and learning shows a depth of love within your marriage. It shows you care. It shows your dedication to this lifestyle, supporting him as his wife. Learning small tidbits along the way — rate, rank, physical training (PT) schedules, job description — also makes you more confident as his wife. This confidence translates beautifully into fully accepting your place as a military wife and lessening tension when frustrations arise.

The majority of the time the military doesn't make life easier, and it is natural to want to blame your husband or take your anger out on him. If you commit to learning more about what he does and the way the military works, those frustrating moments will become more manageable. I can confess to taking my frustrations of military life out on my husband more than I should. I know it isn't healthy and he doesn't deserve to be blamed, but he is an easy target. I find I do this most when I don't fully understand the details of the circumstance. If I take time to listen and learn, the tension lessens.

You may never be able to fully comprehend his job description or the military as a whole because there are so many moving parts, but you can give it your best shot. Start with the basics and what is most personally applicable: his MOS (Military Occupational Specialty)/rate/rank and when he is up for reenlistment/promotion. As you come to understand his general timeline, it's also important to know how his specific branch is organized. The names and structure of his chain of command at each new duty station is something to learn as well. With every new move his job description will change slightly. Ask him to explain those changes. When my husband is talking about something going on at work and uses acronyms, I try to lock them in my mind as best I can. It usually takes several repetitions but knowing them makes it easier for us to have conversations in the future. This is by no means an exhaustive list of everything you need to learn about the military, but the point is to learn the things that matter to you and your husband. Remember, you are focused on staying united as a family and creating a solid foundation so you can better find where you belong.

Battle Buddy: Kati

Kati, a Navy wife, is one of the best listeners, which in turn makes her great at learning about people. Watching her work a room in a social setting is like viewing an Olympic sport, and this skill has paid off well for her in marriage. I will never forget her telling me this story about the simplicity of listening, caring, and understanding, which helped make her marriage stronger.

Her husband had been on a deployment in the Middle East. He was away from home for about 7 months, during which he shared an interesting story with her about a cultural celebration he observed. The details aren't important right now, but she digested every single word of what he was telling her at the time. She asked questions, truly caring about his experience half a world away. She was knee deep in all the weird nuances that seemed unfamiliar to us here in the US. Did she particularly care about it? Not really, but she cared about her husband, and at the time, this was important to him. She invested valuable time to hear him out.

Fast forward to several years after this deployment, yes, YEARS! Kati and her husband were attending a military function in a new city with brand new friends. They started down the familiar conversational road of "Where have you been stationed?" and "Do you know so-and-so?" and because the military world isn't so large after all, the deployment to the Middle East was found to be a common denominator among these new acquaintances. The unique cultural celebration weaseled its way into the conversation and Kati's ears immediately perked up. She engaged in the discussion. She was able to ask questions and relate herself and her husband to these new faces.

When the introduction ended and Kati was walking back to her seat, her husband asked how on earth she remembered all those details from years before. He was amazed she paid such close attention to something completely irrelevant to her world. He was proud she was able to regurgitate the story to make others feel welcomed. By doing this, Kati's husband felt supported, respected, and loved. He was comforted by how much she was invested in his work.

In order for our husbands to do their jobs and do them well, they need to feel like we are supporting them, fully invested in understanding what it is they do. They need to feel respected and we, as wives, need to be immersed in their world even though it feels unfamiliar. It might not be the life you thought you would be living, but you must believe there is more to it, and now you need to embrace it. You need to believe in the mission — it isn't just his mission, but your mission.

His job is a lifestyle, not just a means to make money. This job is a calling. It's not for everyone, and for him to succeed, he needs support. That's where you come in, and as his wife, it is imperative you take time to understand the military as a whole and his small part. This happens in the small moments, as Kati's story showed. Your place in his world is found through the seemingly insignificant moments throughout your days as a military wife.

EXPECTATIONS? NO THANK YOU

Mike and I started talking about managing expectations in our *premarital counseling* and we are still talking about it thirteen years later. We're starting to understand that creating expectations of others is human nature, something we need to break ourselves out of repeatedly. It feels a lot like sleep training a baby. You think you've figured it out and for three days life is beautiful. Then growth spurts happen, constipation shows up swinging, and bye-bye sleep. There is no formula for managing expectations within your marriage. But before I dive into what you *can* learn about managing expectations, let's first understand one thing. Prior to your wedding day you had visions, dreams, and desires for what married life would look like. Whether you realized it or not, vocalized it or not, you had a certain hope for your marriage. Maybe you created scenes in your mind based on your favorite movie. Maybe you watched your own parents and vowed to be exactly like them or exactly opposite them. Others influence us all the time and there is absolutely nothing wrong with imagining your married life to be or not be a certain way.

The issue starts to unfold when you allow those desires to turn into expectations. The moment you *expect* your husband to do something versus *desire* him to do something, you are getting yourself and your marriage into trouble. Thinking back to Mike's first deployment, I had a vision of what deployment life would be like. I imagined spending hours at the computer drafting perfectly scripted daily emails, receiving video calls, embracing the "can do" attitude, and powering through the lonely months until we could be together again. The tricky thing about his first deployment was that was exactly how it started. Mike was in an area for a short time where he could call every day and video chat the kids every night. It was amazing to be able to stay in touch daily. As this rhythm continued, I came to *expect* consistent communication as our norm for the next several months instead of being grateful for each moment. All of that changed when his schedule shifted and he relocated. We lost our rhythmic connection times, and I was devastated. I had moved from desire to expectation. It wasn't wrong of me to romanticize deployment life in the beginning — I didn't know any better. The issues didn't begin until the shift occurred from desire to expectation. From that moment on and without realizing it, I had placed unrealistic expectations on him to communicate with us when it was completely out of his control. I became angry and sad, took it out on him, and he withdrew. I let bitterness take residence in my heart and we started fighting from half a world away. I suddenly understood just how hard the next several months were going to be if I couldn't manage my expectations and take every word of communication with a grateful heart.

Giving expectations space to grow within you or your husband can be devastating to your marriage. Have you ever experienced a time when he expected certain things from you? In the early days of my marriage, I kept the house clean and had a hot meal on the table when he got home from work. Please keep in mind, we had no kids at the time, and I hadn't yet found a job at our new duty station. Fast forward several years and four kids later, things started to look different. I could no longer have both the house organized and dinner ready when he walked through the door each evening. It would have to be one or the other, if we were lucky. He had to adjust his learned expectation and understand the reality of our new normal. He might not get either some days, but he began to understand my bandwidth wasn't large enough to hold it all together. We had to have many grace-filled conversations to release these specific expectations from our everyday life.

These may be great examples, but it begs the question: how do you know if your desires have shifted to expectations? One warning sign you can be aware of is when you feel like he owes you. A marriage full of expectations can feel very contractual. If you ever catch yourself thinking your duties as husband and wife should be split 50/50, you may be living within this mindset. A healthy marriage, without unrealistic expectations, is lived best when both partners give 100% and expect nothing in return. This is no easy thing. It takes time to embrace this mindset and I find it becomes a daily discipline to remind myself to expect nothing in return.

In his book *iMarriage*, Andy Stanley says, "One sign that we are placing expectations on our spouse is that we stop serving our spouse." Having a servant heart toward your husband is a sign of health and maturity. You can ask yourself if you are being patient and attentive without an ulterior motive. This is hard, as it goes against the natural thought of "What's in it for me?" Another warning sign of desires shifting to expectations is if you feel obligated to him. Ask yourself if there are times when you feel obligated to wash his dirty uniform, clean out his lunchbox, or even have sex with him. When we notice our mindset stumbling over obligations, we can know they are coming from a place of expectation instead of desire. If you feel disappointed with your husband, this can be a sign of expectations creeping in. You, as his wife, don't naturally choose to feel disappointed in your husband. It's not something you desire from the beginning of the relationship. But if you put expectations into your marriage, disappointment will be your new best friend. Be honest with yourself and search for the root of that disappointment. It may surprise you to find out you have shifted from a place a desire to one of expectation. One final warning sign to look for is when you notice distance between you and your husband. When you rely on expectations to be met within your marriage as the sole means of happiness, you will experience disconnect.

Some of these may be hard to read and others may not resonate with you. There will be seasons in your military life when you will feel immeasurable disappointment.

There will be moments when you feel obligated to the military. There may be moments when you experience each and every one of these signs. Allow me to reassure you, it's normal and there is nothing wrong with you. Managing expectations in your marriage means fighting against human nature. It's not going to feel easy or natural but breaking through into a fresh mindset can ignite a new fire in your marriage, making you closer and stronger than ever before.

If one of these warning signs resonated with you more than the others, pay attention. Ask yourself which one (or more than one) is happening all the time and consuming your relationship. Be aware that these signs are simply arrows pointing to a larger issue — an unhealthy presence of expectations in your marriage. You don't owe each other anything, and if you begin serving your husband without the lens of "what's in it for me", you'll begin to see how living without expectations isn't so hard after all. On a daily basis, I remind myself to love my husband without ultimatums. The goal is an unconditional love between us. Expectations can get in the way and hinder our growth toward loving and serving each other well. This in turn creates tension in my own life and makes me question if I'm really in the place God has called me.

As a wife, I must release control daily. It's in our nature as women to want to control almost every situation, especially within our home and our families. Just as we have to make room for our husbands to reintegrate post-deployment, we must also leave space for him to be the leader of our families. That means unclenching our own grasp and sharing the reins. We can trust that the Lord has created our husbands to be the leader of our families and can trust that when we release control, the world will not end.

As you learn to navigate and let go of expectations in your marriage, you can love your husband unconditionally and without expecting anything in return. As marriages are a union between *two* people, you will have tough conversations with your husband about what it may look like to manage any expectations that have arisen. You can talk about what it would look like for your husband to lead your family and how you can help along the way. You can continue to work at releasing control of every situation within your home and your family. It takes work from both husband and wife; it's not something you can change all on your own. But by having open and honest conversations with each other, your marriage can experience a new level of strength. With that new sense of unity comes a confidence you can cling to as you continue on your journey of finding your place beside your husband in his military world.

KILL RESENTMENT

Our friend Merriam-Webster defines resentment as "a feeling of indignant displeasure or persistent ill will at something regarded as a wrong, insult, or injury". That doesn't sound like the most pleasant emotion, yet here we are stuck in feelings of resentment all the time. I have zero hard facts about this, but it feels like military wives struggle with resentment more than civilian wives. And it would make sense! The military tells us where to go and it may fulfill our husband's sense of purpose, but we are left following along and making the best of what we can. There is always someone else calling the shots, rearranging plans, taking control, and seemingly bossing us around. We feel as though we are living someone else's life. I personally resent that some days, some weeks, and some years. I don't want to feel like a doormat within my own family, so I find myself with feelings of resentment instead of changing my perspective of military life.

One specific season of military life breeds feelings of resentment more than others, and that's during deployments or separations. And while we're chatting about resentment, we might as well bring along its friends, bitterness and jealousy. It's a lovely trio. There was a moment during one of my husband's deployments I remember thinking, "Sweet Jesus, I have to find a way to stop being jealous of my husband." I had received several emails from him with gorgeous scenic photos attached, while also noticing foreign restaurant charges on our credit card. Images of him lounging in the sun on a faraway beach and ordering unique meals formed in my mind. Whether or not they were true images (most likely not), I felt envious of the opportunities he was having versus what I was experiencing at home. I would catch myself thinking terribly jealous thoughts of how he was off having fun and enjoying new cities without having to sleep train children, potty train, etc. Before long, my jealousy festered into resentment and bitterness.

I needed to find a way to start looking at things from my husband's perspective every now and then. I needed to ask myself if maybe he wished he could be home with his family more than anywhere in the world. I needed to mentally put myself in his position and view each situation from another angle. I started thinking about how his love language is physical touch. How hard was it for him to be gone for seven months without so much as a hug? How hard was it for him to be in work mode 24/7 with no days off, no time with his kids, and no one to share new experiences with? In fact, the 2019 Blue Star Families' Military Family Lifestyle Survey found the number one issue of concern for service members was the amount of time away from family. I had created a false reality in my mind during that deployment, allowing lies to become truth, and it turned from jealousy to resentment to bitterness. I had to retrain my thinking because there was a toxicity taking over my body, and if I wasn't careful, it would damage the relationship I had with my husband.

Over the years since that specific separation, I've learned how important it is to view each military scenario through a new lens. It's vital to shift your thinking from "he gets to" to "he has to".

Change this:	To this:
He gets to leave the house every day and talk to real people.	*He has to* leave the house every day and sit through boring briefs when he'd rather be home with his family.
He gets to grab take-out for lunch today.	*He has to* eat out, but I can make something healthy and save us money.

Some days I stomp around my house in a full temper tantrum before I make this shift. Feelings of resentment do not bring out my best behavior and learning to view his military commitments through a new lens is not easy for me. A Proverb teaches us, "A stone is heavy and sand is weighty, but the resentment caused by a fool is even heavier.[5]" The next time you find yourself wrapped up in resentment, remember these are massive feelings. It will take some heavy lifting to shift your mindset and change your perspective, but it is absolutely the healthier posture.

When you are working to kill resentment, practice shifting your mindset from negative to positive — from "he gets to" to "he has to", or "I get to" instead of "I have to". You can also discuss your specific needs during each season with your husband. As this changes with each new

---

[5] Proverbs 27:3 NLT

phase of life and new duty station, it's important to communicate these changes clearly. Knowing how you can help support each other after each new transition will help eliminate resentment taking root. Part of this is being able to name your exact feelings, whether they are stemming from bitterness, jealousy, or resentment. There is power in naming and paying attention to the root of each emotion. Lastly, you can practice immense amounts of grace and gratitude as you work to kill resentment. Remember, this is yet another layer of your foundation to finding your place in his military world. It's unbelievably difficult to lay a solid foundation in his world as a military wife when you are battling resentment about being there.

KNOW THE ROLES

We could create a long and varied list of the so-called roles of a husband and wife within a marriage. The learned experiences of culture and childhood play into perceived roles within a family unit. Although we may create these lists in our minds, there are no concrete job descriptions for husbands and wives. I, for one, am thankful of this every single day as it doesn't confine or limit creativity within the relationship. But it is helpful to understand your role as his wife within each new military season. Just as his actual job description changes with each new duty station, so might yours. There may be a season for him when competition is high for promotion, and you will need to spend extra time and energy keeping things going at home because he is more distracted at work. There may be a time when you choose to go back to school and need him to pay closer attention at home versus his duties at work, giving you space and time to focus on your education. In the seasons when you are raising small babies, it will be all hands on deck to the best of both of your abilities. Your roles as husband and wife need to be pliable and fill each other's needs as circumstances dictate. You live military life together as a unit, so it's important to take time to learn what each of you needs and how it impacts your role within each new transition.

Since military life is lived together, you must take time to learn what would make each of your lives easier and more manageable. There are certain things you can do at home to make his job easier. On the flip side, there are things he can do to make your job at home easier. This may seem trivial, but as women we are notoriously terrible at asking for help. My husband walked into the kitchen yesterday afternoon after working on our sons' dirt bikes and saw a frazzled woman banging pots and pans together in an attempt to get dinner on the table. He immediately understood his role needed to shift and asked, "What can I help with?" He could tell the kids were wearing on me and offered a helping hand. A dozen different thoughts raced through my head of how he could make the dinner process go more smoothly, but I grumbled out, "Nothing. I got it." We do this all the time as wives. As women. We think it is in our job description to keep the home running smoothly all on our own. We let pride take over instead of accepting or even asking for help. As a married couple, it is neither solely your job or his job to keep the house running. It is a part of both of your roles, but in different percentages depending on each season of life. Let's remember asking for help doesn't weaken us. It doesn't make us look incompetent. It's okay to need help.

This specific example works well when your husband is home to ask for help. But what does it look like when he is away for training? This is how military life differs from the lives of civilians. Whether you like it or not, his schedule must come first. The military doesn't leave much wiggle room here. You are committed to submitting to the military, but you must also learn where you fit. Knowing his work requirements from one job to the next will help you define how you fit into the equation. I say "equation" like there is a right and wrong way, but unfortunately that's not true. This is a fluid process, and your role will change with every duty station. When you are working to define your role, you must consider his job first. This isn't always true, but for most situations the military calls the shots. Once you both have a better understanding of what his duties entail and how your new routine will fall into place, you can better define your needs. It's important at each new duty station to clearly state to your husband what you need from him, whether he will be around or not. This may not happen in one easy conversation, but find the time to check back in with each other to make sure your roles are helping to meet each other's needs. It's up to you to define your roles, discuss your needs, minimize expectations, and ask for help. Going through this process will help define your place.

Today's culture and even the Bible have some pretty strong words to say about the role of a wife. It is up to you to be firm in how you want your marriage and role as a wife to look. Remember, you are spending time cultivating a healthy and strong marriage in order to better find your place in his world. If your marriage has a strong foundation, it leaves room for you to spend time standing confidently in who you are as a military wife. If you get intimidated by passages in the Bible like Proverbs 31, be encouraged. Reading lines like, "She gets up before dawn to prepare breakfast for her household and plan the day's work for her servant girls. She extends a helping hand to the poor and opens her arms to the needy. When she speaks, her words are wise, and she gives instructions with kindness. She carefully watches everything in her household and suffers nothing from laziness. Her children stand and bless her. Her husband praises her..."[6] can be overwhelming and leave you feeling like a failure. It is not written to make you chase an ideal model (we'll cover this more in depth in chapter four). You are meant to be hardworking, have strong character, and have compassion for others. You are created to have many skills with great wisdom. Your role beside your husband will naturally include these things as you grow closer to the Lord. And if you can communicate well with your husband your needs during specific seasons, you are on your way to a flourishing marriage and a strong foundation.

DECISION-MAKING

In her book *The Next Right Thing*, Emily P. Freeman says, "...making a living is nothing if you're not also making a life." Just because we have been talking about believing in the mission and building a strong foundation doesn't mean life will stop being lived around us. This

---

[6] Proverbs 31:15, 20, 26-28 NLT

military lifestyle is absolutely our means of making a living, but are we doing our best to also make it a life? The military throws so many obstacles at us that can take our attention away from creating a life we love. We can sometimes find ourselves reacting to life instead of taking action and living unapologetically. Creating a life we are happy with and proud of can be challenging when we are stuck navigating decision-making. This can be magnified during deployments, separations, and transitions.

If you get stuck in the details of a situation or get sidetracked by something the military throws at you, you may project a negative attitude onto those around you and lose the spark of making a life versus making a living. It's important to determine how decisions will be made when your husband is gone in order for the family to stay united and on mission. There is no right or wrong way here and it will absolutely change with each tour, permanent change of station (PCS), and deployment. One of the most important aspects of decision-making will be to make a plan before changes occur. For example, before your husband deploys talk about how decisions will be made and by whom. You can plan to make most of the parenting and discipline decisions because you are the parent at home. But if something more serious occurs with one of your children, talk about how you will communicate with your husband and how a decision will be reached. You don't need to enter into a world of "what ifs" but it is important to have a plan in place for larger decisions versus smaller day-to-day choices. This advice was given to me before my husband's first deployment, and it was extremely helpful. We decided big family decisions still needed to be made together. Our rule was for me to wait to hear back from him until the decision could be made. Sometimes this was inconvenient for the person waiting on the decision, but we stuck to our plan and it helped us live life better instead of living by the constraints of our lifestyle.

We view life this way because we fully believe the husband is the head of the family. It is in the DNA of our family to default to his guidance knowing he has a healthy, loving relationship with Christ. By no means do I wait for him to make every single decision in our family — that's ludicrous. Per our personal convictions and conversations, it is in my role and place as a wife to decide how to feed our family and construct our budget each month. Any decision that will change the trajectory of our family, military career, and marriage comes from the head of our family, my husband. He often seeks counsel from me, his mentors, and our pastor, but I ultimately trust his direction because of his close relationship with the Lord.

There is another aspect to having a plan when your husband is away. He needs to be confident that you can run things when he is gone, but on the same level he needs to know he is contributing to his family throughout their experiences even though he isn't there. Even if he is several time zones away, it is important for him to feel connected. If you have never thought about something like this before, start with a simple conversation. As husband and wife, you can prepare for as many questions and decisions ahead of time as possible. This takes some forethought, so give yourselves time. Consider looking through your family calendar together before he leaves on a deployment and prepare for upcoming events. Within this conversation, ask him what decisions are important to him. You may think he doesn't care about which doggy daycare your dog will visit when you are working, but he may want to help make that decision. You'll never know if you don't ask. Creating a plan for decision-making means you must, as the wife, let him lead. You must let him make decisions from afar and not assume he is too busy to care. You must include him in the big family decisions while allowing him space to lead. If he truly is unreachable or too busy, you can set boundaries for what to worry him about versus what to handle yourself. It all comes back to having an open line of communication between the two of you and trying to prepare ahead of time as much as possible. Even if you know what is best for you and your family while he is away, still consult him to make sure he feels included. What works for me or for someone else may seem crazy to you, and that's okay. Find a system that works for you and your family. You will find it gets easier as time goes on, but this is especially important to understand in the beginning days of living military life together.

WORDS MATTER

One thing to keep in mind as you work toward a solid foundation is how your time in the military isn't only influencing the people within your four walls. Of course your military experiences impact your nuclear family. Being a military family absolutely shifts who you are as a person and the perspective you keep as you walk through life. But those changes impact more than just you. Throughout the journey, you will meet thousands of other military wives, church friends, community members, the list goes on. How you act, what you say, and the posture you hold impacts each of those relationships. What you say about your husband's service will influence every person you meet and their perception of the military. Your words matter.

As kids we were taught that sticks and stones were the only thing that could break us. We all now know how powerful words can be — uplifting or devastating, life-giving or soul-crushing — and there are consequences to go with them[7]. We must be mindful of how we speak, especially regarding the military and its impact on our families. If we, as wives, believe we are here to be our husband's helper, then we must also realize our words must match this belief. Our words must match our posture as we walk through military wife life. Our words must reflect the changes we are trying to make as we learn to find our place in what feels like his world. During difficult seasons, it is easy to complain to everyone around you. It can feel therapeutic to vent to a friend, but grumbling to an acquaintance shows an attitude of discontentment. If you spend your time nitpicking every decision the military makes for you, it will cast a negative light on your lifestyle. If you whine on social media about your husband or the military, you are inviting bitterness to enter your heart as you also set a poor example to those around you.

Another military wife friend asked me a great question the other day. She said she noticed the environment within her home seemed to rise and fall with her attitude and the

---

[7] Proverbs 18:21 NLT

words she chose to express her moods. She asked if the same was true in my home. Once this truth was illuminated for me, I couldn't unsee it. It is absolutely true. If I grumble to my husband or my kids about our next set of orders, the kids start to take on the same stance. On the flipside, if I get excited about future changes, our children and even those around us reciprocate the higher energy and get excited too. It is true within our homes and the relationships we hold with others. If we follow this thought even further, we will learn a valuable lesson as military wives. What we say directly affects how well our husbands can stand in their purpose to serve this nation.

The next time you are about to complain, grumble, or bash the military or your husband's unfair schedule, think carefully. Ask yourself if what you are about to say will help or harm your husband's time in the military. Our God is a big God and He can handle your frustrations. Take your pain and hurt to Him, and speak kind and uplifting words to others. When working on using words wisely, you can start within your own four walls by complimenting and staying positive when military plans change. This will help unite your family as you live out your military lifestyle and others will take note when they hear less negativity coming from within. Let's be honest, complaining publicly isn't a good look. It will be ridiculously difficult to find your place in a world you continue to be bitter about on social media. When you are committed to the mission, it must be seen in everything you say and do. You aren't putting on a front outwardly, but are doing the hard work to inwardly to change your perspective of what it means to live military life as a united family.

Battle Buddy: Jessica

Jessica, an Army wife, admits it can be easy for her to slip into the mindset of "It's not fair!" There was one deployment specifically when she had to remind herself of the unified mission over and over again.

Her husband was overseas in Kuwait while Jessica struggled to keep a healthy perspective at home. Within the first few weeks of the deployment, they found out they were pregnant with their second child. On the heels of celebrating new life, they were faced with the news of Jessica's grandmother suffering a massive heart attack. Pregnant and with a toddler in tow, Jessica traveled to be with her family. Weeks later she watched as her grandmother passed away. Knowing that her grandfather would need help grieving and transitioning, Jessica made the decision to pack up and move several states away. Living in a new area and dealing with a deployment, pregnancy, and loss, Jessica had to shift her perspective. Wasting her time complaining about her situation wouldn't serve her well. Little did she know just how tight she would need to cling to her belief in her family's unified mission.

Whether it was the stress, grief, or simply her body giving in, Jessica went into early labor while carefully navigating her grandfather's transition. A Red Cross message was sent, and her husband was flown home for the early birth of their baby girl. Two weeks later, her husband returned to Kuwait to continue serving our nation. As if all of this wasn't enough, a major heart defect which required open-heart surgery was found in their new daughter, and another Red Cross message was sent. The Army was able to send Jessica's husband home a second time, just in time for his daughter's surgery. Jessica remembers thinking many times, "If only he had any other job."

This story is a reminder of how much sacrifice it takes to make the mission run in a unified manner. Jessica and her husband have two healthy kiddos and continue to serve this nation proudly, but we can learn so much from their experience. The hard truth is our husbands don't have "any other job". They have this job and it's important to remember how much of a lifestyle switch it needs to be. People outside the military don't have to worry about Red Cross messages, unstable communication, and intense levels of uncertainty. This way of living will undoubtedly frustrate us, but we wouldn't be living it if deep down we didn't believe it was worth it. As Jessica's story reminds us, there will be a point in our journey when we must remember our husband's calling and our place within this lifestyle. When the storm ripped through Jessica's family, did she throw her hands in the air and walk away from it all? When the stress of deployment and death and early labor wreaked havoc on her weary soul, did she give up? She may have wanted to, but the Lord was writing her story. Deep down she trusted Him, her family, and their unified mission.

BELIEF IN THE MISSION: REVIEW

When you need to accept your lifestyle, you can:
- Embrace the mess (no more divided plates)
- Remember the mission

When working on being better a listener, you can:
- Schedule connection time
- Remove distractions
- Make eye contact
- Refrain from interrupting
- Make physical touches
- Ask about what you don't understand

As you learn to navigate and let go of expectations, you can:
- Love unconditionally
- Serve and expect nothing in return
- Give space to lead
- Let go of the need to control

When working to kill resentment, you can:
- Change "he gets to" to "he has to"
- Discuss specific needs during each season
- Name feelings
- Practice gratitude

When working on defining roles, you can:
- Identify the needs of your husband
- Clearly state what you need from him
- Have the hard conversations
- Ask for help when you need it

When working on decision-making, you can:
- Create a decision-making plan before deployment
- Look at your calendar and prepare for upcoming events
- Ask what decisions are important to him
- Let him make decisions from afar (don't assume he is too busy)
- Include him in big family decisions
- Set boundaries for what to worry him about versus what to handle yourself

When working on your words, you can:
- Think before you speak
- Speak kind and uplifting words about your husband to others
- Compliment your husband
- Refrain from complaining publicly about military decisions (especially on social media)

– CHAPTER 3 –
RIGHT VS. WRONG COMMUNITY

"Building community is taxing, but the work is worth it. We were never meant to go it alone."

— Shannan Martin, Foreword, *Back Roads to Belonging* by Kristen Strong

Support System	52
Characteristics of the *Right* Community	59
Red Flags	65
Do I Belong?	68
Finding Friends	71
Spill the Tea	75
Setting Boundaries	78
Battling Loneliness	80
Made for Right Now	83
Right vs. Wrong Community: Review	86

In a recent interview, Jennifer Goodale of the Spouse Programs Support for Military Officers Association of America (MOAA) said, "If you think right off the bat this military life is not working for me, wait till you get a B billet and your spouse is around a lot more and you find a great community. Be patient." I think we can all agree there are highs and lows with military life. Some duty stations will leave an imprint on your heart so deep it will feel like you are leaving a piece of you behind when you move. Others will drag on and never be missed. But Jennifer highlights such an important part of creating strong building blocks for military wife life. With each change we encounter as military families, there is a part of our experiences that are always influenced by the community around us.

If you've been a military wife for any amount of time, you've probably heard about or experienced the importance of community. But if you are a brand-new military wife, soak up this advice like a sponge. Stay in community with others. Get connected and nourish those friendships. It may be stressed more when facing a deployment, but it is just as important when your husband is home, too. Making friends and surrounding yourself with the right community are the next set of blocks to lay as you learn to live military wife life well. Your strong foundation was built as you understood the importance of a unified marriage, and now you are bringing more people into your close circle to keep on the journey of finding where you belong as a military wife. I'm not sure if you've ever heard the belief that you are the average of the five people you spend the most time with, but I think there is a hint of truth to it. If I am being honest, I think you are influenced by far more than your five closest friends, especially with how much we are linked to people through social media. All this to say, I fully believe community is essential and valuable to enjoying military life, but it's more about the *right* people than the community itself.

SUPPORT SYSTEM

121 days. One third of an entire year spent in bed and on my couch. From my limited perspective, bed rest is the

worst way to be taught endurance but with the most amazing reward at the end. Before we can get to the intensity of bed rest, I should back up and tell you how I found out I was having triplets. It was Mother's Day weekend of 2013. Mike and I were running a 5k for charity and at this point knew we were pregnant, but without a clue it was more than one baby, let alone three. Mike pushed our toddler in the running stroller, and I ran — read: jogged and walked — beside him. Without being able to recall the exact finish time, I can say with certainty it was not completed in under 40 minutes, possibly even 50. I struggled through most of the race even though I had been a runner for a little while. Mike was painfully patient, and our daughter was just excited to get tiny water cups and snacks throughout her time in the stroller. I was frustrated, but chalked it up to first trimester exhaustion and tried not to beat myself up about it. Besides, the race was just the beginning of what was going to be an amazing weekend. We were living in a small town in Nevada, and I was surrounded by the most remarkable group of military wives. My group of ladies met weekly for coffee chats. We watched each other's kids when emergencies popped up. We found ourselves at each other's houses several times a month for dinner. Our husbands got along, and our children adored each other. It was the kind of friendships you dream about or see in the movies. And to get even more idyllic, my post-race plans included a mom's day out at the spa! I enjoyed resting my tired legs poolside as we sipped champagne. We sat in steam rooms and saunas chatting about military life, our hopes and dreams, and asking each other parenting and marital advice. I smile thinking back to that day in the company of humble, grounded, confident, and loving friends. I couldn't imagine anything getting in the way or challenging the strength I felt as I carried new life and having such support within my military community.

Until the next morning when I woke up in a pool of blood.

I would love to say I am exaggerating, but it was one of the scariest moments I can remember. There was so much blood. In hurried confusion, Mike and I dropped our toddler off at a friend's house and rushed to the small community hospital. Though the minutes felt like hours, we dreaded the miscarriage confirmation we expected. I sobbed into my husband's chest as I tried to tell the young triage nurse how many weeks pregnant I was. After a blood draw and much confusion over my elevated hormone levels, they sent me for an ultrasound. The ultrasound technician calmly asked how many kids we already had at home. I remember being confused by this question as my shirt was pulled up and cool goo was spread all over my belly, unstoppable tears streaming down my face onto the crinkly paper beneath me. I mumbled something about having a toddler and the technician smiled as she said, "That's great. I have good news. Your baby is healthy and so are the other two. I see 3 heartbeats. You are having triplets." Instead of tears drying and celebrations beginning, the tears came faster for so many different reasons. Feelings of relief and fear arrived simultaneously. How could I carry and care for three babies and still have time for our toddler? Could we really do this? Questions raced through my mind as the tears kept coming before I noticed my husband shaking with uncontrollable laughter.

Our initial reactions may have been vastly different, but we landed in the same stunned place over the next few weeks and months. We were having triplets. Holy Jesus, how on earth did this happen? How was this possible and what were we going to do about it? How could we afford three babies? The questions never ceased as we processed the news. But before we could find answers to those questions, we had a long, hard pregnancy to survive. We found out I had been bleeding that morning because of a small tear. The babies were growing faster than my body could handle, and this issue would continue to scare us throughout the entire first trimester. I ended up in the ER two more times over the next eight weeks with the same pool of blood threatening my hope of healthy triplets. Eventually the tear healed, and we thought we were out of the woods. However, at 17 weeks, my cervix was measured and declared basically useless. My high-risk pregnancy doctor said if we didn't do something quick, my body would try to go into labor by week 19. This was a scary time, but the right thing for the health of myself and our babies was to stitch my cervix closed and be put on bed rest. The goal was to get to 28 weeks. The doctors were confident they could keep our babies alive if I could make it at least that long.

Let me pause here and take a wide-angle view to this situation. I was on bed rest at home — allowed up to eat one meal per day, shower once per day, and use the bathroom. Outside of those boundaries, I was to be in bed or on the couch. So there I was, totally incapable of caring for my family in a normal capacity. My husband had to work full-time (at least he wasn't deployed) and my sweet two-year-old had no one to care for her all day. We were set to move across the country in the middle of my pregnancy, which was now very clearly impossible. We were asking the detailer to shift my husband's orders around, to do whatever he could to keep us together during this fragile time. We moved to a larger house the month before I was put on bed rest and still had boxes to unpack. Never in my life have I felt more helpless than I did then. Helpless, alone, and scared. And it was right here, in the middle of my perceived misery, that I understood how valuable a healthy community can be in times of need. I wish I could say I endured 121 days of bed rest with grace, but I was miserable, short-tempered, highly emotional, and as my mother would lovingly say, a complete grouch. It's all true. I was not in a good place. But with the selflessness of our remarkable friends and family, we made it through and have three healthy triplets to show for it.

My forced dependency on others reminds me of a story[8] about a paralyzed man and his four friends. One day there was an opportunity for the paralyzed man to be healed, but he had no way of getting to the person who could heal him. Without hesitation his four friends carried him, on a stretcher of sorts, to the house where the healer was staying. On this particular day there was a massive crowd lined up outside the house. The four friends, desperate to help their friend, climbed to the roof and began to dig. Yes, they tore a hole through the roof of the house and lowered their paralyzed friend down into the home on his stretcher.

---

[8] Mark 2:2-5, Luke 5:17-26 NLT

They stopped at nothing to see their friend healed, even when the friend couldn't do anything to help himself. The man was indeed healed, but only because his friends had faith.

Have you ever been in a situation where you feel like the paralyzed man — desperately in need of help but unable to do it yourself? Maybe you feel like your whole world is hard to navigate because you can't do it all on your own. Maybe you are physically ill and unable to care for those around you in the way you wish you could. Maybe your mental state is too fragile right now and you desperately need assistance but aren't sure where to turn. Or you despise asking for help, so no matter the struggle, you suffer in silence. The goal is to find the kind of friends who know you well enough that you don't have to mastermind the plan for yourself. The goal is to have the kind of friends who will carry you when you are weak. The goal is to have the kind of friends who will cook for your family when you are on bed rest. The goal is to have the kind of friends who will lower you through the roof, for the love. The goal of stepping into the right community (versus the wrong one) is to have the kind of friends who will stand in the gap for you when your faith feels nonexistent.

The paralyzed man needed help, healing, love, and support. But he couldn't do it alone. He had a group of people around him who shared his passion and goal of wellness. They sacrificed their time and resources in order to see it through and find healing for their friend. What an amazing act of friendship, loyalty, and faith. There's something worth talking about here. In a society where we so badly want to do everything ourselves, we are forced to lean on the faith of others to make it through the hard seasons. I physically could not make meals for my family. I physically could not change my older daughter's diapers. I physically could not carry out my daily duties as a mother and wife. Sure, I was taking great care of the three babies inside of me, but there was a feeling of failure when it came to taking care of the rest of my family. I had to lean on the faith of my friends during this season because I found myself sinking deeper and deeper into a dark place of self-loathing and negativity.

Our support system during this time became the faith we needed to carry us through. My mother and mother-in-law worked out a rotation to sacrifice time with their commitments and work to fly to Nevada every two weeks to care for us. Our military friends brought us dinner each and every week. A hair stylist friend came to my house to make sure I felt beautiful with fresh haircuts and pedicures. Our church family checked in via text and house calls. We had countless people praying over us around the clock and in dozens of states throughout the US. The *right* community is a force to be reckoned with in times of need. I was not strong enough to make it through this lonely, dark season by myself. I fought to accept that, but as I laid in bed day after day, I understood what it might feel like to be the man on the stretcher. I needed help and my next right thing was to accept the help and faith of my friends. Without their support, unwavering love, and unshakable faith, the 121 days of bed rest might have left me in a depression so severe I don't want to imagine how different life would be. But because of the community around us, I delivered three amazingly healthy triplets at 34 weeks 6 days and brought them home from the NICU only 16 days later. It's an amazing testimony of how a remarkable, healthy, faith-filled community can help one individual through an extraordinary time.

And let's not forget, it is because of an amazing support system that our husbands can continue to do their jobs well without worrying about us. Besa Pinchotti, Senior Director for Advancement at the National Military Family Association (NMFA), says, "when a family is well supported the service member can focus on the mission at hand" and it is so true. Mike's commanding officer was very generous, but Mike never had to worry about balancing work and the high-risk pregnancy his wife was enduring. He leaned on the strength of our family and friends just as much as I did. It takes dropping our pride and accepting help. It takes releasing the control of how we think and expect things to go. It takes a posture of gratitude. But when we can align all these things and lean on the faith of a support system, miracles can and will happen. Your support system matters for you, your family, and the overall mission of your military life.

CHARACTERISTICS OF THE *RIGHT* COMMUNITY

I am a confirmed and embarrassingly habitual spiraler. Most everything in my mind intensifies quickly and I jump to conclusions without knowing facts. I know this about myself and yet it still comes as a shock when my best friend calls to talk me out of worrying about things beyond my control. Not that I am speaking from experience, but it might be probable for me to think we are entering financial ruin when the preschool announces a tuition increase. Or for me to fully believe I'll never make new friends at a new duty after one failed coffee chat. Or for me to think my marriage is ending because of one terrible deployment. I can take one hit of perceived negativity and continue downward until I think I'll be broke, friendless, and divorced. See what I mean by spiraling? It's a steep and icy slope for me.

Those closest to me know the tools I need to stop the spiral. But it wasn't until I let people in and prayed for deep relationships that this was possible. Before I understood the power and influence of others in my life, I had friends who encouraged the spiral — who would toe the line of insanity with me and then push me over the edge. I've experienced both and I can now say with confidence I want the friend who calls to remind me of God's promises versus the friend who calls to play the "what if" game with me. There are times in military life when I can't see the other side of the mess. Whether it's tuition prices, moving, or deployments, I now know the importance of having a proper support system.

There is a difference between the right community and the wrong one. I won't say every military wife wouldn't help a friend or neighbor on short notice, but it takes intentionality and discernment to guard your heart against the women with unsuitable intentions. The right community consists of those who challenge you to be better and will help with the big and small parts of your life because they truly care about the success and health of you and your family. No one is perfect and friends will make mistakes, but it's important to look at the character of your core community. You want the ladies who will hold you up when you can't stand on your own two feet. Ladies who pray for you in the good times and the bad. Ladies who cheer you on. Ladies who hold your hands and let the tears fall when you can't see through the darkness. Ladies who cook your family dinner. Ladies who ask for help from you when they are in need. Ladies who you can call in the middle of the night. Ladies who love you for you.

The right community is invaluable. When the uncertainty of military life strikes, you can feel confident your strong and *right* community can lead you through. You will be able to lean on their faith when you don't have enough of your own. But maybe this isn't your reality right now. Maybe as you read this you are realizing there may be people in your life who don't have your best interest in mind. Maybe you are realizing you need friends like this in your life but don't know where to start or how to make that happen.

There are several common characteristics within healthy communities, and it's important to understand what those are as we bring new friends into our circle. If we look at a community of people thriving, we can see characteristics like hospitality, helping those in need, contentment, healthy marriages[9], boldness, and fairness[10]. It may seem obvious to surround yourself with ladies who value hospitality, but I know sometimes we can get comfortable. Sometimes the struggle to find your person is exhausting. And when you do finally find her, you stop

---

[9] Hebrews 13:2-5, 15-16 NLT
[10] Proverbs 28:1,3,5 NLT

inviting others in. It's important to have a close circle, but it is equally important to keep the invitation open. It takes quite a bit of courage to follow through on showing hospitality, on being invitational, and on helping those in need. Yes, of course we want to surround ourselves with the right community, but that also means we must bear these characteristics ourselves. I am guilty of thinking about inviting the new family over for dinner but never acting on it — never once considering that maybe that wife is in the middle of her own spiral, desperate to feel accepted. There comes a time when you have to stop making excuses, stop running away, and be bold. Being bold as you live in and search out the right community looks like seeing through the pride your friends may be holding onto. You may have a close friend who says she doesn't need help, but it may be because she thinks asking for help is a sign of weakness. I encourage you to be bold enough to show her love in the form of help. Most likely, she needs it most right now but doesn't know how to ask.

Hospitality, boldness, and even fairness are all obvious qualities to look for in friends. But what about friends who honor marriage? What about friends who value contentment? These might not be obvious characteristics, but they are no less important. Evaluating your own circle is hard work. It's important to not only learn these characteristics but to reflect on your own relationships, past and present. Finding the right community takes an incredible amount of work. Self-evaluation of how you are being a friend to others takes an equal amount of work. Sometimes you may not want to open your eyes to what might be wrong, but you can be assured the work is worth it in the end. Afterall, we all want a friend who, with one simple phone call, can help us believe we aren't going to be poor, friendless, and divorced. That friend is pivotal in helping find your place as a military wife.

Battle Buddies: Claire & Alissa

Alissa and her Marine were facing an upcoming deployment while stationed in North Carolina. Before they said their goodbyes, they attended a one-day marriage workshop with his unit's chaplain. It was at this workshop that Alissa met Claire, the Navy chaplain's wife. Claire's husband, David, was deploying with Alissa's husband and the two women bonded immediately. The marriage workshop laid the foundation for a pivotal friendship.

Alissa was going into this deployment knowing she would be delivering her baby all by herself. She was going to need a strong community surrounding her. Claire, a mom of five, was exactly who Alissa needed in her circle. Alissa's husband was able to watch the birth via video call from David's office overseas and the strength of friendship between these two couples continued to increase. They discovered just how valuable their friendship had become when Alissa was hospitalized with an illness only 11 days after giving birth. The baby wasn't allowed to be in the hospital with Alissa, but Claire was able to jump in and care for the sweet newborn. God Bless the strength of military mamas, right?

While chaos was swirling in North Carolina with Alissa, Claire, and six children, the helplessness felt by their husbands overseas was extensive. David worked tirelessly to get Alissa's husband home. After five days of paperwork and several flights later, Claire placed the sweet baby girl into her daddy's arms for the first time. Not long after his return home, Alissa was released from the hospital to recover at home. Their family was together again after a very tumultuous time, all thanks to a deep friendship cultivated quickly in a time of need. It's a beautiful story of how well our military community can come together, but it doesn't stop there.

As the deployment continued through Halloween and Thanksgiving, Alissa fully recovered with her husband by her side. When Christmas started approaching, Claire found herself feeling run down and exhausted. Truthfully, she had been feeling this way for almost a month, but chalked it up to her busy schedule, the holiday bustle, and the normal stressors of a deployment. This was her family's fourth deployment in five years, and she figured things were catching up to her.

As it turns out, she had mononucleosis and no clue how much it was affecting those around her. Her preteen daughter was so worried that at one point she emailed her grandma for help. Eventually Claire's health became enough of a concern that David started reaching out from overseas — reaching out to command, friends, and family. He was worried about his wife and hated to hear how much she was struggling.

Claire had found the end of her very long rope and her body couldn't hold on. She couldn't care for her five children or make Christmas morning the special time it should be. But here is the most beautiful thing about surrounding yourself with the right community.

In the days and weeks leading up to Christmas morning, countless people showed up to feed Claire, her children, and to care for her family. And at the end of this, guess who made Christmas morning a magical experience for Claire and David's five children?

Alissa, her husband, and their sweet baby girl.

They sacrificed time and resources to make Christmas amazing for Claire and her five remarkable children. Alissa let Claire sleep most of the day while she and her husband cooked, took care of all six children, and celebrated Christmas. Alissa dropped everything to help pull her friend through what felt like an impossible situation. Alissa loved on Claire's family without complaint, just as Claire had done for her only months before.

Both women showed incredible mercy, kindness, and love during their shared deployment. Both women jumped in to physically help in a time of need.

If you have been a military wife for any amount of time, you know how invaluable a friend like Alissa can be; how invaluable a friend like Claire can be. We're better together, when we're connected with the right community.

RED FLAGS

We started reading the Harry Potter books with our oldest daughter when she was in third grade. We are firm believers of reading books before watching movies, so it became a pattern to read a book, then watch the corresponding movie during the triplets' nap time. Over the course of several months, we made it through the Harry Potter journey, both books and movies. It was a great season to go through with our oldest and we have some fun memories of her experience. I didn't intentionally set out to have a mandated third grade rule in our home, but because she did it that way, the younger siblings had to follow suit.

Without paying much attention, approximately 28 months went by and it was then time to repeat the cycle with the triplets. They had not forgotten the third grade rule and so we started the Harry Potter journey once again — books before movies, of course. What was such a magical and new experience for our oldest turned into something slightly more stressful this time around. I had not anticipated the know-it-all attitude our oldest would adopt and how tempting it would be for her to shout out spoilers. I had not anticipated how she would immediately play the one-up game with her siblings as they went through Harry Potter trivia. I had not anticipated her passion turning into a stumbling block for the rest of us.

There are plenty of women in our military wife community that have a poor outlook. I'm not belittling them or saying they aren't justified in their feelings, but that doesn't mean we have to welcome them into our close circle of best friends. These women can be part of our larger circle, but we must be aware who we are letting into our crew of besties. Whether this behavior or attitude is coming from a place of passion or learned experience, there are deeper issues at hand. You can watch for certain red flags as you begin searching for your right community.

If there are people close to you right now who rely on wealth, pride, arrogance, and complacency[11], take caution. If you have someone popping into your book club trying

---

[11] Ezekiel 30 NLT

to play a know-it-all card, take caution. If you have someone one-upping everyone else at your neighborhood block party, take caution. These are red flags that something deeper is happening in their heart. Does this mean you can't be friends with these women? Does this mean my family will have to cast out my oldest daughter from the Harry Potter journey for the triplets? Absolutely not. We are called to be hospitable but there is a difference between showing love to a stranger and finding your people. We must take caution only when we notice others *relying* on these traits time and time again. I can forgive my oldest daughter for her excitement over getting to share her experience with her siblings because I know these aren't her normal characteristics. As her close circle, we as her family can help her see how her attitude and actions are impacting those around her and move forward with grace. And that's the important thing to remember when we are dealing with real people's feelings. We must, in our search for our right community, keep grace in mind.

It's okay to have a few close friends. It's okay to limit who gets how much of you and your precious time. You need those lifelong besties who will carry you through anything. I'm not sharing these red flags to make you put every friendship under a microscope and cut people out because a friend went through a season of complacency last year. No, we will all screw up at some point. We simply must be careful of who we let on the inside and who we love from a distance. Our close people will hurt us sometimes. Our close friends will offend and irritate us. Our right community will mess this up on occasion, but we can easily respond with grace and forgiveness because we know their hearts are right. We know their intentions are pure. We know they care for us because of who we are, not because of what they need in return. Yes, be kind to everyone. Be hospitable. Be willing to serve others. But vet those closest to you because your heart can be fragile. You need to be cautious who you are letting hold pieces of it.

My oldest daughter didn't realize she was hurting her siblings by not letting them experience the joy of something new. She didn't understand how her actions were impacting those around her to feel discouraged about something that could and should be fun. It's no different for the military community. When you meet a spouse at a new duty station and she word-vomits every great and terrible detail about the base or post, it can project her experiences onto your outlook, spoiling the experience for you. It is frustrating, but you don't have to welcome those attitudes into your everyday life. It can be discouraging if you don't have a friend with live-giving characteristics right now, but you must keep in mind you are asking a lot of humans. There has to be self-reflection to determine if your heart is hardened to the goodness of the people around you. Maybe the right people are there, wanting to get into your life, but you haven't been willing to open up. Maybe you are harboring some red flags yourself. If you are doing the heart work and hard work of finding your place, your people, and connecting intentionally, the right community will develop around you.

DO I BELONG?

The Blue Star Families 2019 Military Family Lifestyle Survey found that "35% of active-duty military families have no one in their local civilian community whom they know well enough to ask for a favor." This number is too high. We can try to justify it by saying those families probably have military friends they can call, but the truth is military families are not connecting enough. Finding our people within the military community is great, but there is a whole wide world outside the military that has much to offer. We must not stop searching for our right community even if that means going outside of the military and into the civilian community. We have a lot to offer the civilian world, and while it may be a journey and a process to find those people, we may find our sense of belonging somewhere along the way.

Does seeing the word *belong* send your anxiety into overdrive? Does it leave you with a longing heart? It does for me! I don't think it's presumptuous to say all military wives have struggled with belonging at least once in their adult lives. It comes with this lifestyle and it's a natural part of being a woman. We want to fit somewhere. We crave a sense of belonging. We want to feel like we have a place. This feeling is at the heart of why this field manual exists. I've seen too many military wives struggle to find their place in what sometimes feels like his world. Maybe you can walk into a social event and bounce from conversation to conversation without hesitation or maybe you find your introverted self quaking at the mere thought of walking into a spouse's event by yourself at a new duty station. Maybe you can plant one foot on either side of the introvert-extrovert line depending on your season of life. Regardless of your Enneagram number or personality type, we all feel like we don't belong sometimes.

If you are in a season of frustration radiating around friendship and belonging, you aren't alone. Kristen Strong, in her book *Back Roads to Belonging*, says, "If something doesn't fit within our communities, it's more likely either it isn't supposed to or it doesn't fit yet." Let's all give a big YES MA'AM because this is a truth we all need to keep close to our hearts. Your current season may be transitional, so if something feels like it doesn't fit, maybe it isn't supposed to, or maybe it's the wrong time. You have permission to let it go or pick it back up six months from now. Our Father in Heaven knew this day would come and He isn't surprised. He knows you have a place because He created you to be right here right now. You are seen where you are and there is a plan for what's ahead. If that means standing on the sidelines for a bit, you have to be willing to stand with patience and integrity. But if you are being encouraged to engage, please do not ignore the nudge. You need to show up. You are made to belong, but the path may look more like a mountain switchback than a five-lane freeway.

Will you always feel like leaving the house to go to a new book club? Absolutely not.

Will you search for months to find a place you feel you belong? Sometimes.

Will you sometimes feel defeated? Yes.

Will the fight be worth it? Yes.

I've often found myself asking, *do I belong here?* I do this with military life, church events, our kids' school functions, and hipster coffee shops. It is still undecided if I belong in the latter, but it is a resounding yes to everything else. I know this because I trust the Lord led me into these seasons on purpose and with a purpose. If I trust Him to do that much, I have to trust I also belong. When you search for your belonging place, you must tell yourself you aren't alone. The survey alone says there are at least 35% of us who are in the same situation, though I would go as far as to say any military wife you talk to can relate to a feeling of not belonging on some level. If you can accept you aren't alone in these feelings, let's try taking action the next time you are around others. What would it look like if you left a seat open at your table the next time you showed up to a Bible study? This would leave a wordless invitation to whoever else may walk through the door. What would it look like if you complimented others freely? This could open the door for further conversation and potential feelings of belonging. Some of these may sound hard if you are more introverted, but that only means they will be worth more when you decide to take action. When finding your belonging place within your right communities, you must promise to never give up. These efforts will never be wasted — they are the groundwork for fruitful relationships.

FINDING FRIENDS

As my children have grown over the years and entered elementary school, they

have gone through the typical ups and downs of making and losing friends. Remembering those times ourselves, Mike and I encourage our children at the beginning of each new school year to be open to new friends. Depending on the child this is met with excitement, horror, or indifference. After a year or two of repeating this each

September, one of our sons asked how to make a friend. I was confused, thinking it obvious, but my husband chimed in immediately with reassurances and simple instructions. You see, in my mind this was common knowledge, clear-cut. Making friends was never hard for me. But the boy asking the question is a clone of my husband, not me. Mike started to tell him how when he is making a new friend, he starts by saying hi and introducing himself. Then he asks a simple question to get to know them better. My husband was able to give our son an equation, and having a set of instructions set our kiddo up for success. What I thought was obvious was challenging for him, but with a few clear instructions, he was able to navigate this sticky situation easier. Regardless of if it is easy or not, it's no less simple. We encouraged our son to invite others along during recess if he was playing a game, but we told him if he was by himself at recess and others were playing a game, he would need to be brave and ask to be invited into the circle. We encouraged him to share and be open about friendships, because it's hard being in a new situation, whether it is him or a new friend. I thought about this for a while and realized how making friends in elementary school doesn't have to be different from making friends now.

As parents we can easily break this down for our children to help their entry into social situations. So why is it so difficult when we need to do these things ourselves? Every time you see a new duty station on the horizon, anticipation may come crawling into your stomach at the thought of having to make a new friend. Or maybe you are like me and get excited about new people and new experiences together. Whatever side you gravitate toward, how can we make this transition easier on ourselves and each other? Well, we can take it back to elementary school. We can take my husband's equation and when we are in a new social situation say something like, "Hi, I'm Heather. I'm new here, but I'd love to get to know some people! What is your favorite part about this duty station?"

Say hello. Introduce yourself. Ask a question.

It might come with a whole lot of scary anxiety, but the simplicity stays the same. This goes for both sides of the introvert-extrovert line. Be brave and either ask to be invited in or be brave and invite others in. This is the only way we will continue to grow and cultivate our right community. This doesn't mean every single friendship is going to blossom into a lifelong bestie. In fact, the friends who stay with you forever are few and far between, but that doesn't mean they're not the right friend for the right moment. In the 2020 NMFA Summit, Dr. Howard said, "We all need our support system… our tribe of military spouses." It's easy to agree with her, but it's a topic without a clear solution much of the time. When I heard this, I asked myself questions like:

> *How do I find the right tribe?*
> *Where do I start searching?*
> *Is it worth it?*
> *How long is it going to take?*

Alison, an Army wife, encourages new wives to focus on finding seasonal friends, and I think this holds immense value. As we go through our own journeys of being newlyweds, having babies, and raising toddlers then teenagers, it is important to have friends in the same season. Whether it is for the duration of a duty station or for the rest of our lives, we need spousal support from women in the same stage of life. It doesn't mean we can't and shouldn't have friends who are in every stage of life, but having those friends who are in the trenches with you can and will fuel you when your tank runs dry.

There are many practical things you can do to find friends, and we'll get to those, but let's revisit the topic of grace. If there is ever an opportunity to practice living with grace as a military wife, it is here. Not only showing grace to others as you meet new people, but extending grace to yourself. I could pound this message into my brain with a baseball bat daily and I would still struggle with it. Let's look at it like this: if you feel inspired to start or host a spouse group or Bible study, do not overthink it. Let go of any expectations you may have about your home, your furniture, your knowledge, and your brand of coffee. You extend yourself grace and learn hospitality in the messy middle of life. Open your home, brew the whatever-brand coffee, let the kids run around in their diapers while you throw crackers at them, and have real conversations with real people. In order to gain genuine friends, you must first be genuine and vulnerable. And that's exactly what is at the heart of the simple friend-making equation — your genuine vulnerability to say hello, introduce yourself, and ask to be invited in.

If we revisit the questions I was asking myself during the Summit, we can learn how finding friends isn't so difficult after all, if we know where to look and how to go about it. When finding friends, you can first and foremost embrace a hospitality focused mindset. Your mindset must be postured toward the want and need for the creation of your right community. If your attitude toward making new friends sucks, you'll continue to make excuses as to why it's too hard. Once your mindset is positioned, where do you start looking? My favorite places to find *quality* friends are church, Bible studies, local mom's groups, and through volunteer opportunities either on base/post or at my child's school. If there isn't a Bible study or weekly coffee chat available in your area, consider starting one! Do the brave thing and invite others into your circle. Remember, you aren't alone in thinking you don't have a belonging place. The last things you need to keep in mind as you create new friendships are to promise yourself to never give up and to pray for guidance. You and your family have been sent to this duty station for a reason and you can trust the Lord will see you through to your people. Finding your place in what feels like his world requires you to be brave, extend grace, and trust the process. But you can do it because you know you are purposed for military wife life and can't do it without a healthy community surrounding you.

SPILL THE TEA

I get so excited when the text comes through from my best friend, an "OMG" followed by the "..." because she is about to unload a juicy bit of information straight to our message thread. At that moment I want to find a place on the couch, kick up my feet, and soak in the drama as we thumb texts back and forth. Give me a bowl of popcorn and I'll take this moment over Netflix any day. Gossip is one of those things we know the "should" and "should nots" of, but rarely do we find ourselves willingly shutting it down. It's the same reason some of us love to secretly check the base/post neighborhood Facebook groups. Those pages are alight with gossip and drama and it's near impossible sometimes to hold back from joining in the fire. I think we love it so much because it provides a distraction from our own story. There are days when I am too stressed, bored, overwhelmed, or lazy to work through my own mess, so I live for a good text message rant or someone to spill the tea online. I know it isn't healthy, but I'm a curious human with zero discipline sometimes. It's hard not to engage. I want to be able to sift through the details of someone else's drama and insert my opinion to make myself feel better. Except when I'm on the other end of the gossip — then I desperately wish everyone would stop talking and continue on with their lives.

    I can remember a time like this for me in high school. Thinking back to these years feels like I am staring at an eel trapped in a too-small glass box. From the outside looking in, it is hard to tell where one end starts and the other stops, but the squirming is hard to watch. I was dating a guy, not my husband, and we got caught making out in the back of my car one weekend. (Side note: why didn't anyone tell this country girl that police cars patrol city parks after dark?) The cops took full advantage of this as a teaching opportunity and took us back to the station. They made me sweat it out in a small interrogation room before finally releasing me to my irate parents. I was horribly embarrassed and devastated. I was such a "good girl" and to have something like this happen was mortifying. Of course, the rumor mill started in our small town and at school, but no one quite knew the full story, as things typically go with gossip. I walked into school Monday morning with my head down, trying to make myself invisible against the endless stares and whispers. It felt like everyone had heard a different version of the story.

What was a dumb mistake turned sinister because people felt the need to talk about what they knew, what they heard, or what they thought they understood. Some assumed I was pregnant, others said I was arrested. I spent so much time in the bathroom crying that first week back I can't believe I didn't get called to the office for skipping class. Gossiping never does anybody any good. Ever. It's hardest on the person or people being gossiped about, but it also steals the attention and energy of others. It's not life-giving. It's not pure. It's not lovely. It's not kind. It's not honest. It's not admirable. Nicky Gumbel, pastor and author, reminds us "that whoever gossips to you will probably gossip about you." We need to think before we send those texts, before we add to the comments section. Are we keeping our thoughts fixed on what is true, honorable, right, pure, lovely, admirable, and excellent[12]? If we can't answer yes to all, we need to keep our mouths shut.

I got nothing more than a reprimand from law enforcement that weekend. My parents took my car away for a while and I endured plenty of embarrassing lectures and conversations. But the story at school writhed around itself and squirmed in every direction. It became crystal clear that week who my *right* community was, and who didn't belong in my close circle anymore. Some of the

---

[12] Philippians 4:8 NLT

people I thought were my best friends were the ones spreading the most gossip. It was a couple of true friends that held me as I cried in study hall who never said anything to anyone.

When you are tempted to gossip, you must be honest with yourself and ask why you are sharing this specific information. You can even flip that around and ask someone else why they are telling you something. Looking at the motive behind sharing information within your community is important when determining where you belong. We want to be like the study hall friends — the ones who let others vent without spreading it to others. As awkward and unnatural as it may feel at first, you must become someone who shuts down conversations heading in the wrong direction. You must be able to click away from a toxic thread. If you feel it is your place, you must be the one to stand up for another even when mistakes are made. The more you can get into healthy habits regarding gossip and drama, the more you will attract your right community.

SETTING BOUNDARIES

Being a military wife comes with its own set of struggles, and being a military wife living overseas is an entirely new experience with its own challenges. If you have children, you may find yourself raising them in a completely different culture while you're trying to acclimate to the newness of everything around you, all while simultaneously making friends. Sounds like a recipe for stress. Consider Morgan, a Navy wife, who found herself in this exact situation when stationed overseas with her husband and two kids. Once they started to get settled, she began the search for friends and her right community. She met a fellow American family and was initially excited to bond over their shared circumstance. While it started off great, Morgan felt unsettled within the friendship as time passed. Morgan started to notice how her friend continued to get more needy as the months went on, frequently asking to drop in and let their kids play together or wanting to spend weekends together. Morgan soon discovered how vastly different their parenting styles were and how their spiritual beliefs didn't align. In a different season of life maybe Morgan wouldn't be bothered by this, but her husband was gone a lot during this time and she was busy homeschooling her young children through the weekdays. Weekends were sacred at her house so they could come together as a family and reconnect. Morgan found herself questioning the health of her friendship and wondering if she needed to set some boundaries.

We all come across differences in our friendships. Whether it's a disagreement about parenting styles, the way you cook, or the schedule you keep in your own home, we are all human and have differences. It's what makes our communities so vibrant and alive. It's what makes each friendship unique and treasured. But it's hard work cultivating healthy relationships in the midst of our differences. Issues within friendships start to arise when we have a hard time setting and keeping healthy and appropriate boundaries within our own families and friendships. While yes, we are talking about creating a healthy community around you, your first and primary focus is that of your family and your marriage. Regardless of your physical circumstances, the health of your familial relationships come before your right community.

If you, like Morgan, have friends blurring those boundaries and knocking on your front door every week, demanding too much time from you and your family, you may need to set healthy boundaries. This can start with a simple conversation where you explain your need for boundaries during this season of your life. If the friend still isn't respecting your request, you can limit your social events together to public places instead of meeting within each other's homes. Meeting in a park instead of your living room creates a buffer but still allows for the friendship to be explored. This can also help keep a manageable time limit on the outing. If the issue persists, you may need to exercise your no muscle more. A simple no, coming from a place of love, is okay! You don't always have to say yes just because someone asks. As you are planning your days and weeks, you can be sure to reserve one night every week to stay home — a mandatory reset for the entire family. This will help the rhythm of your week in addition to staying connected when schedules are jammed.

Ultimately, not all friendships are long lasting. Some friends are needed in a specific season and others will pass through after one or two coffee dates. This is okay as long as you are aware of the impact your friendships are having on the people in your home. You'll know you are on the right track toward your right community when your requests for boundaries are granted with respect and a smile.

BATTLING LONELINESS

It was Mike's second deployment, and I was surrounded

by four small children. They always found me no matter where I tried to hide to sneak a candy bar. The noise was inescapable. I received endless hugs and snuggles. Belly laughs had me grinning from ear to ear each day. The tantrums drove my blood pressure to new heights. I was outnumbered and surrounded, and yet I felt incredibly lonely. At the same time, my friend down the street was experiencing her very first deployment. She and her husband had no kids and she came home from work every day to an eerily quiet house. She played music and watched TV to fill the emptiness she felt within her home. We had vastly different circumstances and yet we both felt loneliness tugging our hearts.

Loneliness creeps into the lives of every military wife whether we have children or not. We can experience loneliness in a crowded room or alone on the couch. Unfortunately, it isn't a feeling solely dedicated to showing up when our husbands leave. Before we look at how to battle loneliness, you first need to understand a few things about the feeling of loneliness and the physicality of being alone. Emotions or feelings, by themselves, are not bad. Sometimes we confuse this truth and think we're doing something wrong because we feel a certain emotion. We aren't. The issues start to unfold when we take those emotions and start to believe them as a truth in our lives.

Just because you feel something, doesn't mean it's true.

My friend and I felt lonely when our husbands were gone, but that didn't mean we were alone. Emotions, while they aren't bad, aren't always trustworthy. There may be something happening deeper. When you feel lonely, you need to ask yourself why. Sometimes the answers can be found in naming the source.

Why do you *feel* lonely?

Is it because the love of your life is halfway across the ocean?

Is it because you are distanced from your extended family?

Is it because you just moved to a new state?

What is making your feelings of loneliness magnified right now?

Sometimes laying it out for your eyes to see is all you need to realize your feelings of loneliness are valid and true, but there's something deeper underneath. It's okay to feel lonely because of what is happening all around. What's not okay is attaching loneliness to your identity and staying stuck in your emotions regardless of your circumstances. Once you do the hard work of naming the source, the answer to loneliness lies in taking action. It takes real work to battle loneliness. It takes courage and boldness. You must put on your big girl panties, take a deep breath, and take action.

No one around you knows you are lonely unless you tell them. Be courageous and vulnerable.

No one around you knows you need to set up a playdate to keep yourself sane unless you tell them. Be courageous and send out a few text messages to other moms in the area.

No one around you knows you need help painting your living room unless you tell them. Be courageous and ask for help.

No one around you knows how much your quiet house is eating away at your nerves. Be courageous and invite a friend over for dinner.

No one around you knows how lonely you feel when he is gone even if you are surrounded by children. Be courageous and intentional about cultivating deep friendships.

Fighting back against loneliness is not easy. The answers may be simple and easy to read, but taking action is hard. Taking action might look like sending that SOS text to a friend, connecting with other military wives in your same season, going to church, looking for volunteering opportunities, or seeking professional help if you've tried everything else. You may feel loneliness during a deployment or during a training exercise but there are others around you feeling the exact same. Just because you feel lonely doesn't mean you are alone. Loneliness will always be a part of our story as military wives. When we can walk together with vulnerability you can come back to those feelings of loneliness and stand in the freedom of your right community. You must be able to feel the loneliness, acknowledge and name it, but not let it consume a part of your identity.

MADE FOR RIGHT NOW

We've spent the previous sections in this chapter talking about your right community as if it is something that already exists. We've talked about seeking it out and finding those life-giving people to surround yourself with. You may be thinking there is a group currently in place with which you can easily fit into. This may indeed be true for you right now, but it may also be true that you need to create your own right community. In a recent interview, a

Marine Corps wife named Grace said it beautifully, "There won't always be a sense of community right off the bat unless you go forward and find that community for yourself." There may be scattered people all around you desperate for someone to bring them together, desperate for belonging and friendship.

Regardless of whether you step into or originate your right community, there's one truth you need to know about yourself. You were created for a purpose, on purpose, in this exact moment of time. When the world was formed and the Lord saw all of eternity before Him, He knew that you, just as you are, would be perfect for right here, in this year, with these people around you. You weren't meant to live in 1743 or 1915. You were created for your existence in this moment of time. If that doesn't rattle your soul and make you feel significant, I don't know what will. Knowing just how timely your existence is and how there is a greater plan for your life, you can rest assured your right community is here if you're willing to put in the work. You are here for a reason with the people around you, but that doesn't mean it's going to be a path without detours. You will experience speedbumps along the way that may hinder you as you continue to cultivate your right community.

It is one thing to know and believe you belong, but taking action requires an entirely new skill set. You can believe something without putting it into practice. But you aren't here to ONLY change beliefs. Yes, that is part of this process, but by now you probably know I'm a person of action. I want you to believe the right community is invaluable and then I want to see you living it out with your friends, old and new. There is a unique strength in you which can only be uncovered by your right community. You need them as much, if not more than they need you. They will be your accountability, your strength, your cheerleaders, and your supporters as you find your place in the military wife world.

RIGHT VS. WRONG COMMUNITY: REVIEW

When leaning on the faith of others, you can:
- Accept help
- Release control
- Stay grateful

When evaluating your right community, you can:
- Search for those mirroring hospitality, boldness, a healthy marriage, and contentment
- Live your own life with upright character
- Reflect on previous friendships
- Learn from past hurts

When watching for red flags, you can:
- Focus on attitudes passioned with arrogance, pride, and complacency
- Evaluate with grace
- Self-reflect

When finding your belonging place, you can:
- Tell yourself you are not alone
- Leave a spot open at your table
- Compliment others freely
- Promise to never give up on your quest for belonging

When finding friends, you can:
- Join a local church
- Embrace a hospitality focused mindset
- Join or start a military wife Bible study

- Find a local mom's group
- Volunteer
- Promise to not give up
- Pray for guidance

When tempted with gossip, you can:
- Ask "Why are you telling me this?"
- Let friends vent but not spread their stories to others
- Stop conversations or change the subject
- Walk away
- Defend the person or subject being gossiped about

When setting boundaries with friends, you can:
- Limit social events to public places
- Exercise your "no" muscle
- Set time limits for play dates
- Reserve at least one night per week for a family night

When navigating feelings of loneliness, you can:
- Send an SOS text to a friend or family member
- Connect with other military wives
- Go to church and engage
- Look for volunteer opportunities
- Seek professional help

– CHAPTER 4 –
IDENTITY MATTERS

"Your wellness is worth your time because you are in a service lifestyle."
— Kimberly Basco, military wife and founder of InDependent

Time to Mourn	92
Proverbs Model	96
Wellness Routines	100
Morning Routines	102
Evening Routines	107
Sleep Struggle	109
Daily Affirmations	115
Stay Committed	117
Identity Matters: Review	123

During one of my husband's deployments, I found myself spiraling further and further into a toxic routine. It's not as though I woke up one morning and decided to live as a shell of myself, but little by little over the course of a few months I began to barely recognize my life. Allow me to bring you into one of my more glamorous nights. I was drenched in a pool of sweat, heaving a fancy steak dinner and vodka tonics into the toilet bowl at 2:30 a.m. Cute, right? Now that you have that image burned in your mind, let's look at how I got there. The evening before, my military wife besties (notice how I didn't say my *right* community) and I decided a casino night would be a great idea. We hired sitters for our combined dozens of children and hit the town. We dressed up, did our hair and makeup, and pressed pause on our normal lives. This wouldn't have been an issue, and I would even encourage this level of a girl's night out every once in a while (minus the part with your head in a toilet), except this wasn't an out-of-the-ordinary event. This had become my norm.

The wives and I had a fantastic time. We grabbed drinks before dinner as we chatted about how great it felt to be out sans kids. We treated ourselves to the best restaurant in town. We ordered more drinks with dinner and even more as we danced through the casino shoving money into slot machines well into the small hours of the morning. We spent a night out escaping the busyness of deployment life and numbing with alcohol and an expensive meal. Watching everything come back up with the sourness of regret brought me back to the reality of my situation with sudden alarm. As I sat on the tile of the bathroom floor in a cold sweat, I knew I could no longer let this deployment be dictated by the back-and-forth of casino nights and wine nights disguised as book clubs. I had four tiny kiddos sleeping down the hall who needed more than a hungover mother while their dad was fighting for our freedoms.

In the moments leading up to my unraveling, I saw absolutely nothing wrong with how I was living. In fact, nothing immediately changed after that night. But the memory remained and as time went on, I never forgot how I felt that night on my bathroom floor. Looking back now, I see a broken wife, a hurting and lonely woman who craved identity and worth. I see an exhausted mom who turned to TV shows and alcohol as a means to numb the pain she didn't know how to process. I see a military wife who was consumed with resentment and bitterness toward her husband. I see a military wife who wasn't taking care of herself on almost every front. It's hard to think back now and admit how much I was struggling, but that's exactly the reality I was living in.

At some point we all hit a hard place feeling lost, confused, and lonely. For me this happened not one time, but several times over. It wasn't always obvious like alcohol abuse, but as I look back, I can see pain at each duty station. I remember feeling overwhelmed in Florida and pouring my energy into a full-time job. I remember feeling confused in Nevada as we grew our family and I grieved the dream of being a working mom. I remember feeling angry in California as I cried alone in an empty apartment. I remember feeling lonely in Mississippi and turning to alcohol. I remember feeling resentment toward my husband in Virginia as he thrived at work and I stayed home with the kids. We will all have moments when we feel like we are barely surviving. It's easy to sacrifice our own health and wellness, especially when our husbands are gone, but there is something much deeper to consider.

Yes, the bad days will happen. The ground beneath our feet will falter. The feelings we have toward military life will shift with every season. But here is a beautiful truth to cling to: though we carry on through these changes and feel unstable, our identity *can* stay intact. When you place your value and worth on external variables, your mental state suffers. The longer you are in this military lifestyle, the easier it becomes to adapt to the changes around you.

Easier to adapt, yes, but not easier altogether. Turning to alcohol, friends, or social media will feel good in the moment, but those will never get you closer to accepting your true identity. Clinging to girl's nights and vodka tonics to see me through a deployment was inevitably going to lead me to the bathroom floor because I was holding onto the wrong anchor point.

Your reaction to military life is not a direct reflection of who you are as a woman. You are not defined by how well you handle certain seasons of your life. Your identity, who you are and who you're meant to be, lives much deeper than surface-level circumstances. Let's pause and be incredibly grateful for that!

So you reacted poorly when you heard where your next duty station was. That's okay! It's all about living a grace-filled life and you can move forward knowing your identity lives much deeper than one poor reaction.

So you totally crushed it as the secretary on the Family Readiness Group (FRG) board and now you feel the pressure to be all in all the time at every duty station from here until retirement. No ma'am! It's all about living a grace-filled life and you can move forward knowing your identity lives much deeper than the high expectations you are putting on yourself.

Military wife, you are where you are supposed to be right now. This truth may excite and empower you, or it may hurt like a thousand knives in your chest. Either reaction is okay, but it doesn't lessen the truth behind the statement. Your identity does not rest fully on being a wife or mom. You are a whole, complete, capable, and equipped woman of God outside of your role as a military wife.

Yes, serve your husband well as a military wife.

Yes, create meaningful community as a military wife.

Yes, preserve hope within your military family.

But do not doubt your wholeness, identity, and calling outside of being a military wife. Cultivate who you are at your core by being aware of what brings you joy. Take care of your mind, body, and soul so you can love who you truly are. When you learn to accept your true identity and step into military wife life as a whole, complete woman, your life and the lives of those around you will radically change for the better. Your place in his world is not limited by the confines of the military.

Up until this point you've done a lot of work on those surrounding you – your husband, family, and your right community. This is all necessary as you continue to add building blocks to your life, but the real strength comes from the work you will do within. This is some of the hardest work and may take the longest, but without the loving support of those around you, it wouldn't be possible. God created you to be where you are and He knows you are capable of doing the hard and heart work as you find your place.

TIME TO MOURN

Before we get into the details of what it really looks like to take care of yourself as a military wife, we need to pause and mourn. You absolutely can't skip this step. I went to college as an honors student in engineering, studying biomaterials with dreams of inventing new cardiac stents. Thirteen years later I am a stay-at-home mom of four, learning to serve my military husband as we travel around the world together. We have come to a place of fully believing this is where we are supposed to be, but that level of acceptance did not happen overnight. What happened to my education and my dreams? What happened to my sense of purpose and identity after four years of pursuing a career? What happened to my mindset once I realized my plans didn't align with God's plans? We'll get to those answers, but first you must understand there is an important piece to mourning and grieving your felt losses. There are many things you might pursue in life that aren't right for you. There are opportunities that may fall into your lap that invite you into something you never saw coming. Regardless, you must be okay with taking time to grieve the loss from one season to the next.

It is okay to feel sad about losing what you thought was your dream job, dream house, fill in the blank. Your soul needs to heal and you don't need to apologize for needing time. I had to take time to mourn the loss of my education. I had to take time to mourn the loss of my career goals. I had to take time to learn to love my new role as a stay-at-home mom of the small army I helped create. And it wasn't one day of grieving, no, I still take moments to mourn the loss of what once was. I have to remind myself I belong here. I know I am allowed to be sad about what I had to give up to be here, even when I can't see the purpose behind it. It's okay to be sad even though you made the right decision. You have permission to rage. You have permission to let tears fall. You have permission to sulk. You do not, however, have permission to be afraid. Change can feel big, scary, and downright wrong sometimes. We both know how much we have to deal with change as military wives, but you must not fear what's in store for you and your family.

Kristen Strong, in her book *Girl Meets Change*, writes, "In the deepest parts of my soul, I know change is an absolute provision of God's grace. Change isn't something to be feared or dreaded. It's just the next step, his next best thing for you." I haven't counted for myself, but I've heard it said the words "fear not" are in the Bible 365 times. You have an entire year's worth of encouragement to live without fear of what comes next. You are purposed for right here, right now. The change will come. The grieving will happen. But your importance in your family's equation will never falter. You matter. You belong. You are vital. You are essential.

Where we can find ourselves in a sticky situation is how long we allow ourselves to sit in the mourning process. We are military wives and there isn't always time to sit with our box of tissues. We have babies to raise and fundraisers to organize. We have deployments to prep for and plans to execute. I was 30 years old when I received some of the best advice in the arena of grief. It may sound crass, but a friend told me to put a time limit on my pity party.

When you move to a new place, put a time limit on your pity party.

When your husband doesn't get the orders you both wanted, put a time limit on your pity party.

When reintegration gets ugly, put a time limit on your pity party.

It doesn't mean after three days you can no longer feel angry or after two weeks you can no longer cry. What my friend advised was to be fully immersed in your feelings of grief for a period of time. For big things, give yourself more time. For small things, a few hours or days will suffice. But for those hours, days, or weeks, fully feel every emotion. Give yourself time to process the mourning. Don't try to stuff it away or squash your feelings. Let everything bubble over. But on hour four or day three or week two, you must dust off your boots and begin living again, even if it is in the smallest way possible. Yes, still process your emotions as they come in waves, but life must keep being lived. Your family still needs to be taken care of. Your husband still needs to be supported. Your work is not finished, and you can continue with living even in the midst of change.

Put a time limit on your pity party.

You may sink low in the hard moments but having an end date to your sulking gives hope for your weary soul. We sometimes think taking care of ourselves is eating salads and running, but transformation happening inside is the most vital of all. Throughout your times of mourning and moving on, you'll find clarity and peace. These building blocks make for a strong foundation to carry with you into future seasons of change.

Graduating with my engineering degree and moving seven states away with my new military husband consumed my emotions. I never gave myself time to mourn and grieve my losses. I stayed swept up in the newness of military life until I realized how difficult it would be to hold down a job when we were set to move every 18-24 months. Not only did I not put a time limit on my pity party, but I carried it with me for years. Without knowing it, I had wrapped my identity into my perceived failure as an engineer. My mindset turned dark and angry when I spent too much time thinking about what I had to "give up" to follow Mike in the pursuit of his dreams. I carried the bitterness and resentment with me. It wasn't until our sixth duty station, after carrying failure, bitterness, resentment, and my pity party all those years, that I realized I needed to empty my arms and root my identity in something deeper than my circumstances. This process started with grief and mourning. Once I admitted this, I discovered what I thought was failure was simply a new and fresh vision in my life — a renewed identity. I couldn't get to this place without first naming my emotions from all those years ago, giving myself lots of grace along the way, and creating space to feel all my feelings with a time limit. Having my right community surrounding me during this time was truly invaluable, and that's one of the reasons we work to build that foundation before doing much of the inner work. Your identity matters but you will find yourself hitting a roadblock if you try to find your place without first taking time to mourn.

PROVERBS MODEL

When I first read Proverbs 31 as a wife, my jaw just about hit the floor. Now, keep in mind I am an Enneagram 3, also known as "the Achiever" type, so it may not surprise you to hear I had great amounts of anxiety upon learning all the things I was supposed to be doing as a wife. I'm a list maker through and through. I like to check boxes and complete meaningful tasks. It's in my nature. So when the literal Word of God tells me I am supposed to rise before dawn and organize my day, I take it word for word. I'm actually good at these two things, so not a big deal for me.

When it tells me I am supposed to shop around for quality home goods, I'm on board. When it tells me I'm supposed to plant a garden, things get a little more questionable due to my lack of growing skills, but I don't back down from a task. However, I start pumping the brakes when I read how I'm never supposed to be spiteful or worry about my family. A groan escapes me when I read how I'm supposed to face tomorrow with a smile.

It's a good day if I can do one of the things listed in Proverbs 31, but trying to handle it all with grace and elegance every single day? I'm out. I even tried to knit once. I lasted maybe 47 minutes before my fingers cramped and my shoulders were touching my earlobes. Hello, it's the 21st century. I am not mending my family's clothes. It's why we have online shopping. I will never ever in this life be this woman. Never. Let's take the pressure off.

What I've learned over the years as I studied this passage is that the Lord didn't keep this part in the Bible to bring shame upon our lives. He doesn't have this chapter included in Proverbs to make us feel less than. This isn't the be-all-end-all of Christian wives everywhere. We must take the airplane view of this woman's life. We must ask ourselves what characteristics we could see in her if we were a fly on the wall in her home. She's obviously very kind. She's gentle. She's loving. She's joyful. She lives with peace as she goes about her day. She is for sure patient. She'd have to be if her kids are blessing her! My kids mostly just roll their eyes at me. She has an incredibly good heart. And gosh, her self-control is something to be admired.

The Proverbs 31 woman lived before Jesus came to walk the earth. She lived before the Holy Spirit was sent to aid Christ's followers. She knew her Father in Heaven would take care of her and her family, but she also understood her role was vital. Because of this knowledge and understanding she was able to live with the same qualities the Holy Spirit can produce in us. It's fascinating to see the parallels, not the exactness, of how she lives with each and every fruit of the spirit. The Proverbs 31 woman isn't the exact model of who we are to be as women or as Christian wives. She is a woman demonstrating what our lives can be if we are filled with the Holy Spirit, confident in our places as wives, and sure of our identities as daughters of the King. Her daily routine required her to mend, cook, plant, and work. It required these things because of the time she was living in. Your routine will absolutely take on a different hue, but you can model yourself after her by the way in which you do these tasks. Going through your day filled with the Holy Spirit will absolutely help you live with "love, joy, peace, patience, kindness, goodness, faithfulness, gentleness, and self-control.[13]"

There are many things the Proverbs 31 wife does because she has to. But do you notice the things she does for herself? Her self-care looks like knitting and sewing and enjoying the things she gets to do with those skills. Her entire day isn't made up of things she has to do for everyone else. It says she *enjoys* sewing and that she makes her own clothes. Yes, she makes clothes to sell and brings an income to her house, but she is doing something that brings her joy.

---

[13] Galatians 5:22-23 NLT

Can you look at your life and say the same? Are you finding things throughout your days as a military wife that bring you joy? Things you are proud of? Or are you consumed with the trials of military life and allowing your identity to be rooted in your husband's calling? It's not easy to feel the pressure of being your husband's helper while also being your family's caretaker. One lesson you can take away from Proverbs 31 is how much value there is in living a life rooted in Christ while also embracing self-care. Your husband needs to know you are fully healthy and capable of running the household when he is away. You can make that a reality when you live with Proverbs 31 characteristics while staying grounded in your identity in Christ.

The temptation is to focus on our circumstances and make excuses for ourselves because of what life looks like on the surface. The temptation is to attach our identity and our worth to the challenges of military life. The model shown in Proverbs 31 gives the perfect guide to combat those temptations. When you are working to find your place as a military wife, you can lean into this model not as a checklist, but as an awareness of the improvements needed within your character. How do you go about making these changes in your daily life? You first and foremost pray for the Holy Spirit to invade your life, your home, your space, your days. Pray daily to be filled with the Holy Spirit and for him to produce his fruits in you. Trust your husband to be united with you as you seek to root your identity in something more than your ever-changing circumstances. Rely on your right community to help navigate living life within the Proverbs 31 model. Shift your perspective from checking boxes to living with grace. You can do all these things because you know God wouldn't have put you here without fully knowing you are capable of handling it with His help.

WELLNESS ROUTINES

When our triplets were toddlers, I found myself feeling ragged and exhausted. It was a slow decline, but before I knew it, I was drinking a pot of coffee every single day. I was skipping meals because I prioritized my kids over myself. I snitched crackers from their snack cups and counted it as lunch. I put their oxygen masks on before mine, instead of the other way around. After months of this routine, I reached a point when I needed to ask for help. It was hard to admit I was struggling, but with the help of my right community and an eating plan, I slowly found my way to wellness in that season. Years later, after yet another move and more transition, my wellness struggles had nothing to do with food and caffeine, but with my mental state. I was fighting a war in my mind as I tried to discover where I was headed and where I fit in. These mental battles manifested into physical ailments, and I soon found myself unable to prioritize wellness. I quickly learned just how interconnected everything truly is.

When we read the word "wellness", there is the temptation to think only of healthy foods and fitness routines. But as I discovered, there are many more aspects to wellness, and I will be spending the next several sections shedding light on ways to stay healthy and whole as a military wife. Our unique lifestyle brings its own challenges, and we need to equip ourselves with the right tools for this journey. Our minds, physical bodies, and emotions each require specific and tailored care.

My wellness routine has shifted over the years as I've learned more about myself and what I need, but I try to stay consistent in several areas. The things that are life-giving to me, like reading my Bible, working out, and making to-do lists to clear my mind, may not work for you. There is no one-size-fits-all recipe for wellness. It's all about what your mind, body, and soul need within each season of life, including where the military leads your family.

If you are going through a particularly horrible time, seek help and make an appointment with a counselor. In addition to having your right community at your side, it's important to be able to admit when you need more. And that's okay.

If you are full of energy and feeling great about military life, start a walking/running group to help lead other wives through their own wellness journey. Be a light for someone else who may not even realize how much help she needs.

The important thing to remember about wellness is how much learning is involved. Just like there is no formula, there is also no overnight fix. It can take years of learning your own body, your own triggers, your own mind. The benefits are absolutely worth the process but give yourself grace along the way. Take action in your wellness, but also take time to learn. Your physical, spiritual, emotional, and mental routines will change right along with the changes in military life. What works now might not work two years from now. But if you prioritize learning and diligence, health and a return to wholeness will follow.

With each passing season there will be new areas to tend to. With each additional struggle you must take time to learn, adapt, and overcome. You must do the hard work because you are essential. You're essential to your husband, your family, and your community. The journey to find your place within military life is impacted by the belief you have in yourself and how well you can learn to care for yourself. Things like sleep, exercise, drinking water, eating clean, therapy, journaling, and rest are all pieces of wellness routines. Taking time to work on your own mental and physical health isn't selfish, it's imperative. You can't wholly show up for others if you don't first show up for yourself.

MORNING ROUTINES

My mom, like most, loves to tell stories about my childhood. My children beg her to tell them embarrassing tales and she indulges them without hesitation. There is no shortage of material to pull from, especially when she is purposefully trying to make my cheeks flush. But every so often she will tell a story that shocks my kids to their core because it is so unlike the mom they know.

If you were to see me sitting at a coffee shop today, you would immediately learn several things about me. I carry a tote bag with my four favorite things printed on the outside — Jesus, donuts, my family, and early mornings. If you would continue to get to know me for any amount of time you would learn how true this list is, especially that last one. The quiet, early hours of the day are my absolute favorite and those that know me understand how much I treasure and look forward to that time. My husband knows this. My kids know this. My friends know this. It's so important to me I had it printed on a tote. So naturally, it comes as quite a shock to my children when their grandmother tells them stories about how much I hated mornings and her many unique, varied, and repeated ways of trying to wake me up for school throughout my high school years.

She tried everything to get me to wake up on time, but nothing ever worked. After she would pull every last blanket off of my bed, I would roll to the floor and fall asleep among the dirty clothes. When she would try a different angle and bring me breakfast in bed, I would eat with my eyes closed and immediately fall back asleep once I was finished. I hated mornings and nothing was extreme or enticing enough to make me want to wake up before noon. I'm not sure when it changed or how, but over the years I've learned to treasure the early hours before the chaos of my day starts.

Maybe you can relate to me today, or maybe you are like 15-year-old Heather. If that's you, go ahead and roll your eyes to get it out of your system. I'm sure you are ready to flip to the next section, but hear me out. I'm encouraging you to challenge the narrative you have playing in your mind right now. The one that's telling you "you can't wake up early". There is so much freedom to be had in the morning, in the small hours of the day. Not every season of life affords you the margin to wake early — that is okay. But just because you can't right now doesn't mean you can't ever. When you get to a place of being able to start your day before your family, let's look at what a morning routine can look like and how you can create one you love, one that works for you.

Like any other new endeavor, we must start at the

beginning — waking up on time. In the book *The Five Second Rule*, Mel Robbins gives us a new way to think about getting out of bed in the morning when we really don't want to. For those of you addicted to the snooze button, this is for you. Mel pictures getting out of bed like a rocket launching. A rocket has a countdown before launch and when the clock runs out it has no other choice but to blast off. It can't second guess the decision. This is the mindset Mel recommends. She hears her alarm go off in the morning and counts down: five, four, three, two, one in her head. When she says one her body has no other option than to get up and get moving, just like a rocket. This method works great, but I like to add another element to it, especially during times when I have zero self-discipline. I keep this rocket mindset, but I also move my phone or alarm clock to a different part of our bedroom. I place it somewhere I can't reach so when the alarm goes off and I do my countdown, I physically have to get out of my warm cozy bed to turn it off. Once I am up and out of bed it is much easier for me to keep going instead of falling back asleep. The high school version of me never learned this mindset, but I am thankful I have these tools now.

If you have never created a morning routine, start here. Give yourself the goal to simply master getting out of bed at a certain time. Don't add anything else until you are confident you can wake on time and with a purpose. Once you have this mastered, you'll feel empowered to make your mornings your own. I used to think there wasn't any point in creating a morning routine unless I woke up at 4 a.m. with a massive checklist to accomplish before the rest of my day began. I was so intimidated I never wanted to try. I soon discovered even a mere 20 minutes would give me the slow, intentional start I needed. This is where I suggest you start. Set your alarm 20 minutes earlier than your normal wake-up time. If you have a full-time job, try waking up 20 minutes before you have to start getting ready for work. If you have kids to get ready for school in the morning, try waking up 20 minutes before they pop their little eyes open. Moms of tinys, you may not have this margin if you are waking up four times each night to feed and change your babies. This is okay, but take note because this is the gold you will need for your next season.

When you wake up to work emails or needy children, you are immediately reacting. There is no mental or physical preparation for your day. There is no preventive care. You are reactionary right away. You are letting your tiny humans or angry coworkers set the tempo for your day. When you can give yourself even 20 minutes before the kids get up or before your work routine starts, beginning the day on your own time and on your own terms, it is magical. You are taking a stand and creating a healthy atmosphere for you, your family, your home, and the rest of your day. You get to choose how the day begins instead of immediately reacting to other people's demands.

You may be thinking, Okay, great Heather, this is sort of making sense, but I'm just not a morning person. I function better at night. And besides, what do you even do during those extra 20 minutes? I sometimes wish I was able to function better at night and ditch the early morning thing, but in truth, the concept of rising early isn't mine. It says in the Psalms[14] to rise early and give the first part of your day to the Lord. If there is only enough time for one thing to happen in the first few minutes of your day, let it be focused around this idea. Spend time with Jesus. Giving the first part of your day to the Lord isn't merely a suggestion. If you wake up immediately reacting to every situation before you've had time with Jesus, your soul isn't being well taken care of. You're trying to do everything in your own power. But if you connect with Jesus before the crazy starts, invite him into your mess, and ask for the help of the Holy Spirit, imagine how empowered you will be to take on the troubles of your day. The demands of your children or your boss won't feel so jarring if your soul has had time to be postured toward grace. Nothing will be able to stand against you because you'll have the full strength of the Lord in and on you. So, what if you don't have a morning routine you love? Will the Lord never help you in your time of need? No, not at all. You can go through life never cultivating your relationship with Jesus in the morning, but why try to go it alone? He is offering himself to you each and every morning so that he can help you throughout your day, with your kids, in your workplace, with your husband, all of it. He wants to help, but you have to invite him into your space.

There is no one right way to start your day. Start with Jesus, yes, but then there are so many other things you can add into your morning routine to make it something you truly love and look forward to. If you don't make it your own and it isn't something that brings you joy, you'll never

---

[14] Psalm 59:16, 119:147 NLT

stick to it. Once you have your foundation laid — waking up on time and inviting Jesus in first thing — the rest is entirely up to you. For me this looks like feeding my soul with things that are life-giving to me. I like to journal, work out, make my to-do list for the day, and listen to worship music. Before modeling your morning after mine, look inward. Think about what you need right now in your life. Ask yourself what your soul and body need each morning and create a routine you look forward to. Maybe it simply looks like drinking your cup of coffee while it is hot and listening to an uplifting or motivating podcast. Maybe it looks like spending time in prayer and reading scripture. Maybe it looks like cleaning up the house so your mind feels more at peace. Maybe it looks like creating your weekly meal plans and chore lists. You do you, but trust in this small building block as you work to find your place.

EVENING ROUTINES

I recently stopped in my Instagram scrolling when I saw Emily P. Freeman, author and podcaster, talking about evening routines. I thought how interesting it was that we don't see this discussion nearly as much as we hear about morning routines. It's only fitting we follow our previous section with a discussion on evening routines. Emily brought up an excellent point in her podcast when she said it's not that we need to *create* an evening routine. We already have one, but we may not like it. As I started thinking about it more, I realized the only way we can set ourselves up for success with a morning routine is to get to bed on time the night before. Following this observation, I noticed something in my own life. As a mom I made sure to create a bedtime routine for my kids that sets them up for success, but I hadn't done the same for myself.

My children's bedtime routine looks like this:

6:15pm All screens off, begin bath time for all four
7:00pm Straight into pjs, brush teeth, brush hair, lotion, all the necessary hygiene things
7:10pm Pile into the girls' room for a book
7:20pm Bible and prayer time
7:30pm Go potty one more time before bed, tuck everyone in, sing a lullaby

We have stuck to this nighttime routine every night for over nine years and it works great. We have four excellent sleepers. We have four well-rested kids who rarely struggle with anxiety. We have almost no issues waking everyone up in the morning for school. We've put in the work for almost a decade to create a healthy wind-down routine for them and the benefits are visible. I had to ask myself, if I'd put in all this work for my kids, why hadn't I done the same for myself? Why do I value my sleep, health, and wellness less than theirs?

In her podcast, Emily recommends trying a ten-minute routine to close out your day. Ten minutes of being intentional about shutting things down, slowing your pace, relaxing into a posture geared for sleep, and responding to what your body needs. When developing what this can look like in our own lives, she advised we try adjusting our current routine and tweaking small things to start. She said to ask yourself what your body needs before making any major changes. For me, this means not eating anything after dinner. It means not taking my phone to bed. It means keeping the lights in my bedroom low while I'm getting ready for bed. It means reading a chapter of a novel before bed to take my mind off my to-do lists. It means saying a quiet prayer of thanksgiving.

When I can do these things and find this rhythm each night, my mornings are easier. I'm able to feel more grounded and at peace as I go through my day as a military wife, even when uncertainty tries to derail my mindset. Finding and developing these routines have helped settle my soul into a posture better suited to finding my place as a military wife. I know I'm doing something for me, bettering my own wellness, and that trickles into shifting my mindset toward one of gratitude and acceptance.

SLEEP STRUGGLE

According to the Blue Star Families 2020 Military Family Lifestyle Survey, only 38% of active-duty military spouses get enough quality sleep to feel like they can function effectively. The next time you go to a small group function within your military community, know that six out of ten women sitting in the room struggle with getting enough sleep. The reported national average of women in the United States in 2020 who sleep less than the recommended seven hours per night is only 35% according to the CDC. That means twice as many military spouses struggle with sleep than civilians. The numbers are almost the exact opposite! If we start dissecting this and thinking about why sleep is a greater issue within the military community, we start to develop an alarming list. Obviously with major disruptions like deployments, it's hard to adjust.

I can remember having to force myself to go to bed during deployments because nighttime felt incredibly lonely. Nights were a stumbling block because I struggled to find balance between sleep and doing time zone math to be able to video chat. Whether it's loneliness or communication struggles, going to bed on time when your man is gone is hard. On the other side of the deployment, learning to sleep beside your husband again after so many months apart is difficult, too! Sleeping alone for weeks or months on end becomes the norm and then all of a sudden you have to adjust to having another human beside you, usually putting off massive amounts of body heat. It's not easy.

Not only are deployments tough, but our husband's work schedules are rarely predictable. There have been seasons in Mike's career when he is coming and going at weird hours with a work phone ringing all hours of the night. This makes it incredibly difficult to fall into those life-giving morning and evening routines. And if you have a family, you'll have the sleepless nights of motherhood adding to the sleep struggle. Not only are the kids waking you up throughout the night, but it gets tricky to have alone time with your husband. Our only alone time is after the kids go to bed, and if we want to take advantage of that, we sometimes push our bedtime back later. Combine all of this with anxiety or health issues and it's amazing any of us are sleeping at all. This isn't solely specific to military wives, but it's important to bring to the conversation. Health issues play a big role in your ability to sleep. I strongly encourage all wives to talk to their Primary Care Manager (PCM) about how their health and/or medications are affecting their sleep.

Within this same vein, things like stress, worry, and overthinking are big red flags when it comes to sleep patterns. It's no secret our husbands have stressful jobs sometimes. As wives, it's in our nature to worry about and care for our husbands. We want the best for the ones we love and it's hard to calm our nerves. Some feel worried when their husbands work late, so they feel the need to stay up to make sure he is safe. Some feel like they can't turn their brain off when their head hits the pillow and feel like they have to always be doing something. This leads to anxious thoughts, resulting in very interrupted sleep. Some have endless to-do lists racing through their minds at night, leaving them feeling restless. There is no shortage of things we must handle as military wives, and some of us allow the uncertainty of military life to keep us up. When we are in seasons of waiting on orders or promotions, it's extremely hard to turn off the "what ifs".

There are countless worries that may consume your mind at night. I've found it takes vigilance, acknowledgment, discipline, and prayer to fight back against the sleep struggle. During one of our seasons of waiting on orders I found it extremely hard to quiet my mind enough to sleep soundly without worrying about what was next for our family. I felt like I tried all the things to cultivate a peaceful evening routine. I was diligent to put myself to bed early enough, but nothing seemed to work. I had to get really honest with myself and name my worries, my concerns. I continued with my evening routine and made sure I wasn't spending too much time on social media, but I added a short mantra to my bedtime prayers. Each night I released my worry and concern to the Lord — I had to do this nightly because I spent all day carrying around those worries — and repeated God's promise of sweet sleep[15] to myself. It wasn't an immediate fix, but the more I released the need to control the uncontrollable and stood on His promises, the more settled I felt. Soon enough I was back to sleeping soundly even though our orders hadn't been cut yet.

My place during that season wasn't to stress about what was next. My place as a military wife was as a patient example to our children and a grounded sounding board for the countless conversations happening with my husband. In order to be these roles, I needed to be sure I was taking my wellness seriously and getting enough sleep so I could show up for my family. The struggle for sound sleep is real and worth every ounce of effort to overcome.

Battle Buddy: Alison

Alison, in her early twenties, married her husband on a sunny afternoon in June. She kissed him goodbye as he left for deployment in the heat of August in the same year. For the next twelve months

---

[15] Proverbs 3:24 NIV

her abrupt introduction to Army wife life was shocking. She explains it like this:

> *"I was thrown into military life literally overnight. We were married on a Saturday. I moved to a new town on Monday, registered for DEERS [Defense Enrollment Eligibility Reporting System] on Tuesday, and then went to a spouse's day that afternoon. We were thrown into this community and I didn't know what to expect. But I knew I was in love with my husband and this was the career path he had chosen."*

Alison's first year as a military wife paralleled her husband's first deployment. There was no tiptoeing into her new life. She pulled her knees to her chest and cannonballed into the deep end. In an effort to find strength in the midst of a hard deployment, Alison opened her eyes to some of the more difficult parts of her days in order to cope healthily. At the time, she was a full-time elementary school teacher, so her days kept her busy. Evenings and weekends were more of a struggle, so she dusted off an old workout DVD she found in her cabinet. She started exercising daily, mostly in the evenings, to fill the void. She also made it a point to get together with other military friends each week to watch favorite TV shows. She focused on what she knew would help her care for her soul during the long months of feeling isolated and alone. She started taking care of herself through wellness and her right community.

There was no massive turning point for Alison, but small, intentional adjustments each and every day that led her to learning how to get through a long deployment with luster. It wasn't just about surviving a deployment, though. These tools stayed with her throughout dashed dreams, multiple cross-country moves, and raising babies as their time in the Army continued.

Following that first deployment and eventually receiving new orders, their time at their first duty station came to an end. Alison was forced to quit her teaching job — one of the things she had clung to as part of her identity when her husband was gone. After all her years of higher education training to be a teacher and the years spent investing time and talent into the lives of children, she had to say goodbye to that chapter of her life. She felt alone, questioning why she was there and what military life held for her. The Lord created her to be a teacher in the season before, but she was forced to be a fully immersed Army wife now. She was watching as her husband's career flourished and felt like hers was ending. Upon their arrival at their new duty station, Alison found herself without a sense of purpose and facing yet another transition. They would only be at this station for six months. Six months of never feeling adjusted. Six months of questioning her purpose. Six months of feeling unfulfilled. She remembers it like this:

"There was one point in particular in that six-month stint I can remember [my husband] getting ready for PT at 5:30 a.m. I had already been up for twenty minutes pumping for our daughter. I was feeling gross. Post-partum. Not sleeping great. Not really knowing what I was doing with myself. And he sighed and said, "I don't want to go to work." I have never been more mad at my husband than at that moment. I sat up straighter, the hair raised on my neck, and he struck a chord. I thought to myself, how dare you say you don't want to go to work? You get to go to work. Your career is intact. You have given up nothing. I have given up everything. I have given up my career. I have given up my body for our children. I have given up everything. And you have the audacity to complain about going to work and doing something you love every single day. Looking back, it was me feeling unfulfilled, but in that moment, I

was so mad at him for being so selfish about his career and not enjoying it."

After that day, she took time to reflect on what her body needed, what her soul needed. She continued with her self-care routine and gave herself time to mourn what once was and look forward to what was ahead. There was no "aha" moment for Alison, but through small, intentional decisions, she was able to carve out her place in what felt like his world. Through wellness routines and a thriving community, she was able to accept her current calling as an Army wife as she rooted her identity much deeper than what her career may or may not have been. Realizing her calling and place within the military world helped bring Alison out of her frustrations.

DAILY AFFIRMATIONS

One of my favorite and most memorable Christmas gifts from my husband is a small book that fits in the palm of my hand. Inside its pink and red cover are 30 fill-in-the-blank pages. The book is meant to be a display of love between two people in both serious and comical ways. Number ten had him filling out "I really admire the way you _____" but number seven is "If you were an ice cream flavor, you'd be _____, because you're _____ and _____." As I read through each and every statement, I felt tears stream down my cheeks with the chaos of Christmas all around us. I could hardly believe Mike took the time to fill in these pages with such love and sincerity. I read them over and over because I didn't want to forget. I didn't want them to just be nice things he wrote, but I wanted and needed them to become affirmations in my own life. I still keep this small book on my desk and every so often open its pages as a reminder to see myself differently. I use its pages as my daily affirmations when my mindset needs refreshing.

Maybe words of affirmation aren't as impactful for you as they are for me, but don't skip this section. Affirmation may not fill your love tank as Gary Chapman, author of *The 5 Love Languages* series, would say, but they can be a powerful tool in your wellness journey. Having, naming, and repeating these validations to ourselves has recently become almost trendy. I'm praying we see the value in this fad and it gains staying power, unlike POGs and bloody knuckles, two of my middle school obsessions. But what exactly is affirmation and how do you fit it into your already packed days? In my mind, affirmation equals encouragement. Many people will use strong "I am" statements. Others will use quotes as inspiration for their affirmation. Some cling to Bible verses or even words of encouragement from friends and family. Regardless of how you formulate your affirmation, the most effective use of these powerful words is to use them daily.

There are countless ways of incorporating daily affirmation into your routines. My favorite way to bring encouragement to myself is by writing my affirmations on my bathroom mirror. I use dry erase crayons, but dry erase markers work well too. When I wake up each morning, I see positivity and encouragement first thing. I usually repeat them out loud and with purpose. Yes, it's a little bit like being welcomed into Crazy Town, but talking to yourself in the mirror in this fashion is helpful in the long run. Another way to incorporate daily affirmation is with a set of affirmation cards. If you work outside the home, this is a great thing to have on your desk. If you're more digital, there are affirmation apps you can download and try.

As women it's easy to get stuck in our own heads and beat ourselves up for things out of our control. As military wives, we plague ourselves with negative self-talk about mostly untrue things, like how we'll never find our place and never make new friends. There are seasons when you may be filled with resentment toward your husband, stuck in feeling like you gave up everything to follow him around the world and pining for the days when it will be "your turn". Having a positive reminder on your mirror or desk is a great way to turn an about face. It's the act of replacing lies with truth (more on this concept later) and once you can believe the good about yourself and your military lifestyle, finding your place will be that much easier.

STAY COMMITTED

If you've been reading through this entire chapter on identity and wellness thinking how it sounds great in theory but unrealistic in real life, you're not alone. Maybe you've tried some of these concepts dozens of times with little perceived success. Maybe some of them are triggers for you because you've heard it all too much. Maybe you have a hard time believing you are essential because you feel like a failure. I'll let you in on a little secret — I feel this every single day. I battle feelings of failure, insignificance, worth, and value every single day. And if there is one thing God has taught me over the years, it is how I can reframe my mindset from failure to lessons-learned. My mind loves to tell me I can't have a wellness routine. My mind loves to tell me I will never have consistent sleep. My mind loves to trick me into thinking I don't matter as a military wife. But my mind isn't the only decision maker in my life. My heart and the truth I can cling to through Jesus tells me I'm not failing — I'm learning. My heart tells me I can wake up with the Lord and have a life-giving evening routine. My heart tells me I can stand on the promise of sweet sleep. My heart tells me my worth and identity are rooted in Jesus. God can teach lessons on the mountains, but He often does His best work in the valleys.

You may feel like you have tried all the self-care and wellness things ever and nothing has worked. You may be thinking to yourself, *Heather, I've tried running. I've tried getting up early. I've tried journaling and eating healthy and going to bed early, but I can't stick to it. I fail every time.* You may think you know this in your heart, but let me remind your mind: You Are Not a Failure. You are a human, for the love. You are living in a broken world where temptation is strong and very real. Whatever works or doesn't work for you in your wellness routine right now may or may not work for you in two years. Whatever morning routine feels life-giving now may change before the year is up. When you start thinking about taking care of you, back up a few steps from your situation and look through a new lens. You are not the same person you were two years ago, right? So why would the same self-care still work? It's unrealistic to think you can live forever the way you lived in your early twenties, and you need to carry that same mentality through to your routines and rhythms of wellness.

Your commitment to self and soul-care is lifelong, but the methods won't stay the same. If you are a mom of little ones right now, commit to finding time to fill your own soul. If you are a brand-new wife, commit to connecting with other new wives. If you are a mom of teenagers, commit to taking care of you in between chauffeur routes. Your self-care will look different for every season you are in, so when one thing doesn't work or you feel like you've failed, you are simply changing, and that is okay. You can learn from the changes. The next time you start and stop a new workout plan, give yourself a pat on the back for trying, realize you can offer yourself grace, and move on to something that may be more life-giving in your current season. This can be said for almost any new wellness routine or rhythm. When you are trying something new or starting something again, remember to set shorter goals. Staying committed to your mental and physical health is more attainable when the goal feels achievable. Start small and build from a strong foundation so you don't feel the weight of perceived failure if you have to shift things around.

One way I like to keep myself accountable is to plan rewards for accomplishments along the way. I bribe my children all the time, so why not do it for myself? If I stick to a new routine for one week or make that phone call to my therapist I've been meaning to make, I buy myself my favorite coffee or take fifteen minutes alone to read a book I enjoy. This works most of the time, but when I am in a season of low self-control, I make sure I tell someone in my right community to check in on me and keep me accountable. Most importantly when I am working on my wellness routines, I pray. I ask the Lord to help me stick it out. I ask for His guidance on my next right steps as I lean into taking care of me and standing in my true identity.

He's a big God, but He also cares for our wellness and we can trust Him to help us stay committed.

Commitment doesn't mean staying with one thing forever and ever amen. Commitment means never giving up the belief that you are essential. You and your health are essential. You matter in your family's equation, and you do your best work when you are at your healthiest. You must commit to that belief, whatever it looks like for you in each and every season of military life. Your husband needs it. Your kids need it. Your friends and community need it. You need it. Staying committed to your physical, mental, spiritual, and emotional health is essential to finding your place.

Battle Buddy: Kristin

She once believed self-care was selfish, but Kristin went through what no mother should ever have to experience, and fourteen years later, she no longer carries this belief. In the beginning of her time as an Army spouse, Kristin found herself modeling what she thought every military wife should look like. She embraced the challenging lifestyle with an independent posture and an "I can do this" attitude. She made it through their first PCS and was doing her best to transition into their new duty station when she was brought to her knees in grief at the loss of their first child. Their sweet baby girl passed away at one month old.

Kristin barely had her feet under her as a military wife when her world shattered. Everything she thought she knew dissolved. She was left with billions of tiny pieces to put back together and didn't know where to start or how to begin. Within the first year of their loss, Kristin began to see a therapist. Prior to this monumental time in her life, she admits to believing the negative stigma around therapy. For Kristin, taking this step and being bold enough to recognize she needed help was a catalyst to her healing. She recognized how self-care wasn't so selfish after all, especially when in the depths of grief.

After hard soul work, letting the Lord bring his healing hand into their lives, and many therapy sessions later, she started feeling better. She was able to continue on in military life without therapy for a while. But as we know, military life doesn't slow down, even when tragedy strikes. Years later, after more moves, deployments, and two kids, Kristin started to feel like a shell of her former self. She felt bitter toward the lifestyle and her place in it, resentful toward her husband, anxious, depressed, exhausted, depleted, and discontent. She repeated the narrative in her mind, "It's all about him. It's all about his career. He gets all the recognition. I'm stuck at home with the babies. I had to quit my career. I don't know who I am. I'm so sad and lonely. I'm tired of making new friends." Sound familiar?

She knew she needed to get back into a rhythm with a therapist — someone who had the tools she didn't have. Her next right thing for her wellness was to add therapy back into her routine. Looking back on this period of struggle, one tool she still clings to today is how she has control over her thoughts and mindset even when the military makes her feel like she can't control anything else. She doesn't have to repeat toxic thoughts — she can reframe them. Another tool she's kept in her wellness routine throughout the years is journaling. Her journaling practice transitioned from brain dumping on the page to a more intentional process. She finetuned this method and believes in it so much that she now offers a published journal called Life Worth Living.

Kristin's story gives hope that good things can come out of dark places. She encourages military wives, as they begin a wellness routine of their own, to first honor their struggles. Acknowledging that what you have going on right now is hard is a powerful step. You and your self-care are a vital part of your military family, a vital part of finding your place in his world. It's okay to be a beginner when learning how best to take care of you, but don't be afraid to take time and find what works. You and your health are important enough to take action.

IDENTITY MATTERS: REVIEW

When taking time to mourn, you can:
- Name emotions
- Give yourself grace
- Create space to feel feelings
- Have your *right* community keep you accountable

When using the Proverbs 31 model in your own life, you can:
- Pray for the Holy Spirit to live in you
- Rely on your *right* community for accountability
- Shift from a checklist mindset to grace

When creating a wellness routine, you can think about:
- Sleep and exercise
- Water intake and clean eating
- Therapy/Counseling
- Journaling

When developing a morning routine, you can include things like:
- Caffeine
- Working out
- Journaling
- Prayer
- Reading scripture
- Cleaning the house
- Meal planning
- Creating a to-do list
- Listening to worship music or a podcast

When developing an evening routine, you can:
- Set a ten-minute timer
- Make adjustments to current routines
- Ask yourself what your body needs
- Pray or practice gratitude
- Read
- Set phones aside

When you suck at sleeping, you can:
- Get honest and admit why you struggle to get quality sleep
- Create an evening shut down routine
- Turn off screens before bed
- Put yourself to bed early
- Release worries to Jesus
- Stand on the promises of sweet sleep from the Lord

When adding affirmations to your wellness routine, you can:
- Write affirmations where you will see them most
- Buy affirmation cards
- Download an affirmation app

When staying committed, you can remember to:
- Set short goals
- Reward yourself
- Pray
- Ask for accountability

– CHAPTER 5 –
VALUE OF MENTORSHIP

"There are people today who need what you have."
– Russel Brunson, *Expert Secrets*

Needing Guidance	127
Train the Young	130
Made for Encouragement	136
Be Invitational	139
A Good Mentor Listens	141
Confident Leadership	143
Open for Accountability	145
Trust One Another	148
Compassionate Hearts	149
Use What You Have	153
Value of Mentorship: Review	157

When I asked Alexia, a Navy wife, what her biggest piece of advice would be to military wives, she replied, "Finding that mentor and then being able to reach back and mentor the people coming behind you. It's both. Connect with everybody because you never know how connections are going to come full circle and help other people." There are times as military wives when finding friends holds immeasurable value. I dedicated much of this book to emphasizing the importance of your right community. There's one more piece to this concept, though. Within your right community it is vital you find those who have gone before you. It's important to form mentor relationships with more seasoned wives so you can then mentor others. Learning from the ones in front, yes, but then turning around and helping the ones behind. Can you imagine how beautiful military wife community could be if we operated like this?

I used to run track in high school and one of my favorite events was during indoor track season when I got to run the 4x200 meter relay. I was in no way the fastest runner, but I loved the feeling of competing as part of a team. If you don't know anything about track and field relay events, each team consists of four runners. Each person has to run 200 meters, which on an indoor track is one lap. After each person completes their part of the race, they pass a metal tube called a baton to the next runner on the team. This repeats through all four runners until the final runner crosses the finish line. I usually ran the second leg of the race and the baton exchange was my favorite part. I loved being second because I could feed off the energy of our first leg runner, run my 200 meters, and set the next runner up for success as I passed the baton. The baton exchange is challenging because it happens blindly for the recipient. As the first runner is finishing their 200 meters, they must communicate to the next runner when to start running, when to put their hand back, and when the baton is being handed to them. This all must happen in a marked section of only several meters. Did we screw it up sometimes? Absolutely! But we were obedient and open-minded to the overall mission of the race. We worked together to make it happen as best we could.

If we could grab onto this idea through our military

spouse groups, church groups, and community activities, the overall health of military wives would improve. Learn from the ones who have already been running the race, match their pace, communicate effectively, feed off their energy, and run our race strong knowing we can pass that same energy onto the next. If we adopt this analogy as military wives, we are all runners on the same team with a common goal. We are being asked to learn from the mentors in our lives. We are being asked to learn from the strong women who have been living this life longer. We are being asked to learn from their mistakes and not stop there. We must pass the baton.

There will always be someone brand new. There will always be someone who hasn't experienced everything military life has to offer. There will always be someone in need. And you might be the one helping to teach how to run the race well. As you walk through military wife life you must be sure to not take, consume, or live selfishly. You will learn many lessons over the years as a military wife. You can use it all to create a healthier military wife community. Your place as a military wife will take on many forms over the years. It will shift and morph into shapes you can't even imagine right now. Being mentor-minded is but one small piece of your place.

NEEDING GUIDANCE

Merriam-Webster defines mentor as "a trusted counselor or guide" and goes on to define mentorship as "the influence, guidance, or direction given by a mentor". So what do we have if we put them together? **Mentorship is the influence, guidance, or direction given by a**

trusted counselor or guide.

I grew up in a small town in western Pennsylvania. Every summer on the Fourth of July, my family would head into town for the parade. We would always set up our chairs along Main Street, across from the old hardware store. We saw many people we knew as we waited for the parade to start, but I would often walk down a few blocks toward the main intersection. I wanted to make sure I saw all of my friends, and I knew they'd be passing through that specific intersection to get to their own spots. This intersection was always the most crowded location, completely packed with people moving from one place to another. By definition crossroads are a natural gathering place. Some of the people I saw were new and had never been to the parade. Others had been setting up chairs on the same corner for over 50 years. I knew if I stood there long enough, I'd be able to see many of my friends before heading back to my spot.

Thinking back to my small town on the Fourth of July and that packed intersection reminds me of our lifestyle as military wives and families. It's not surprising to see a myriad of people at a crossroad, some you know and others you've never seen before. This is often the case for military wives as we find ourselves in brand new cities and brand new situations. It can be chaotic, loud, and overwhelming. Unlike a familiar small town, we don't always know our way around and may need to ask for directions. But who do we ask? When we're in a new situation or at a new duty station, who do we go to for directions?

Look for the weathered ones in the crossroads. The ones who have already gone down a few of the roads before. The ones with age in their eyes. The ones who have seen this life before. The ones who know the potholes to avoid. Ask them. Ask the ones who have gone before you. Traveling their path leads to rest for your soul[16], but you can only get there if you ask them. You need directions along the way.

As a child who had grown up in the small town, I didn't think twice about walking the familiar sidewalks to the crowded intersection. I didn't need to ask for directions, and it was clear who the new families were. As I was waiting to see my friends and say hello, I would be asked which way the parade would come from and if I knew a good place to set up chairs. I was asked questions because when you are comfortable, confident, and knowledgeable about something, it is written in your posture. We carry ourselves differently when our circumstances and environment are familiar versus when we are navigating something new.

If you're the one carrying knowledge, it isn't always a challenge to share it with others, but when you are the newbie, it's hard to ask for help. It's something women are notoriously terrible at, but something so vital as you continue to mature into your position as a military wife. It's vital you find mentors to help guide you through the busy intersections of military life. Nicky Gumbel says, "There is great power in example. It is hard to improve if we have no other model than ourselves to follow. A good example is not only inspirational, it also gives us a pattern to copy and learn from."

---

[16] Jeremiah 6:16 NLT

When I'm driving through a new town at a new duty station, I absolutely plug the destination into my phone. In fact, it usually takes me several months before I don't need guided directions in a new location. Navigating crossroads on your own can be time consuming and leave you feeling defeated. Having a guide makes each transition smoother. When I am unfamiliar with road names in busy cities, even the GPS isn't as helpful. It's best if I have someone in the car with me who already knows the way. Someone who can instruct me to "follow that white car" or "get in the left lane because you'll need to turn in a half mile". The instructions become the pattern for me to copy and learn from. There will always be wrong turns and missed opportunities, but the mistakes are far less when you have guidance along the way.

Before you can mentor others, you need to first be mentored. It's hard to acknowledge how much help we really need sometimes, but letting your guard down and accepting help is the first step to finding a mentor. You need to keep your eyes open for the weathered ones at the crossroads and follow their lead. There will always be someone who has gone before you, someone who knows the busy intersection well. You can ask for help, guidance, and direction along the way to your own place because without their mentorship, you may hit every crack and pothole along the way.

TRAIN THE YOUNG

Have you had a moment in your military wife life when a friend, possibly a more seasoned spouse, was an absolute lifeline for you? Alyson was that person for me those first months as a new Navy wife. Mike was in flight school in Pensacola, Florida with a fluctuating schedule. I was a brand-new Penn State graduate, job hunting during the day and longing for my place as a Navy wife to be solidified. Alyson was a few months ahead of me in the military wife world, so she became my friend and mentor. She was a stay-at-home mom and because we both had time on our hands, our friendship developed quickly. Our husbands were in school together and soon enough our families were doing life together. We had dinner at each other's houses on the weekends and Alyson and I took her son blueberry picking and to the pool during the week. Alyson taught me all about ranks, promotions, and helped define dozens of acronyms. We chatted about flight school over tacos and how to host a Bible Study as we watched her son on the playground. I can look back on this time and see such fresh ambition in my eyes. I wanted to take the military wife world by storm, but I didn't know where to start. Without Alyson extending her kindness and knowledge, I'm not sure what my story would've looked like over ten years later.

I'm sure you've heard it said that the health of a system is only as good as its weakest part. The military wife community is a system whose health is only as good as its weakest wife. Just like me in Pensacola, there are new wives coming into this lifestyle feeling clueless. There are seasoned wives feeling dejected. There are worn-out wives lost in the shuffle. There are wives desperate for information and belonging but never know where to turn. The health of these women is vital, not only for their own benefit, but for the health of their husband, family, and those around them. It is up to the older wives to help train the younger wives[17]. It is up to the healthy wives to tend to the sick wives. Literally and figuratively. It is up to the more experienced wives to lead the new ones, exactly how Alyson took me by the hand and led me through the newness.

This isn't a new concept by any means, but we don't have a solidified structure in place to keep this model intact. It is up to individual women to see a need and meet it. Sure, this can sound idyllic and nowhere near realistic in today's culture. I am challenging you to change and improve military wife culture. How beautiful would it be to see the older women displaying healthy military marriages? How beautiful would it be to see the younger wives learning from the older ones — learning about love, wisdom, and goodness?

As an older or more experienced military wife, you can first and foremost check your own heart. It's important to ask if you are living a life worth modeling. Are you supporting and serving your husband well? Do you have your right community supporting you? Are you taking your own health and wellness seriously? Have you taken the building blocks talked about in this book and added them to your strong foundation? If you can answer yes to all these questions, there is no reason you can't be mentoring someone in the beginning stages of their own journey.

If you are a new or less experienced wife reading this, you can first and foremost open your eyes. You are in the middle of a busy intersection and need to keep your eyes

---

[17] Titus 2:4-5 NLT

open for the weathered and seasoned wives. Pay attention to how they live, how they serve their husbands well, and how they live military life with grace. Take notes and start to implement these things in your own life. And, as a new wife, never be afraid to ask for help along the way.

Never ever are we going to get wife life right every time. Not a chance. As you move through the building blocks of this book, no one expects perfection. It's a winding journey with plenty of mountain switchbacks and city traffic circles to navigate. As you mature into a more seasoned wife, you can know you don't have to be a model of perfection. A good mentor isn't someone who is flawless. A good mentor learns from her mistakes, leads with integrity, and walks with others through the journey. Does a more experienced wife stand in her cul-de-sac each morning holding a bedazzled sign encouraging the rest of base housing to love their children? She could, but my reaction would be to send my kids outside with her to experience how challenging that is some days. No, you can't just talk about these things and cheer people on from the sidelines. You must live it out. You must be the example. John Maxwell says, "Eighty-nine percent of what people learn comes through visual stimulation; ten percent through audible stimulation and one percent through other senses... what they hear they understand. What they see they believe!"

If your struggling neighbor sees you loving your husband well, loving your children well, and keeping your home orderly, she'll believe you are truly a loving, caring person. Can you put on a front? Yes, but there is a time limit to faking it till you make it. A sincere dedication to your husband, family, and the military is lasting and noticeable. It's the core of your place in what feels like his world. We need to be able to bring forth past experiences and help others learn from our own mistakes. It's a high calling, but we are strong women capable of taking on great challenges.

Battle Buddy: Ashley

When Navy wife Ashley thinks of the word mentorship, three names come to mind: Louise, Janet, and Jill. Shortly after her marriage to a Navy officer, Ashley found herself facing two deployments and a move. After leaving Iraq and returning home, her husband entered a new position on a new base. His job was demanding and left little room for adjustment. Ashley was in a new state with no clue where to turn or how to approach this season of life.

A more seasoned wife, Louise, extended her experienced hand and invited Ashley into a place of belonging. At one particular time, Ashley remembers turning to Louise, her new friend and mentor, and asking, "I don't know what to do. I don't know how to act and I feel like I'm not being myself. What do I do as a military wife, here in this season?" Louise gave some of the best advice that day, advice which has stuck with Ashley for years and that Ashley has passed on to ladies she is mentoring now. Louise said, "Ashley, I always want you to be yourself. Be yourself no matter what. Yes, be respectful, but always be yourself and stay true to who you are." Louise didn't do anything extraordinary for Ashley, but her words have carried Ashley through many challenging times. Louise showed up to Ashley in a big way through what may seem small to the average person.

Ashley's time as a military wife continued and she and her husband welcomed their first baby. In the weeks and months following the birth of their beautiful baby girl, Ashley suffered from postpartum depression. It was through this seemingly impossible time she was blessed with meeting her second mentor, Janet. There are some connections in life that are so powerful, we can't help but fight back tears as we chat about the impact such a person has had in our lives. Janet is this person for Ashley. Through her friendship and mentorship with Janet, Ashley learned how qualities like faithfulness, loyalty, honesty, respect, and care mold a person into an outstanding mentor. Janet would chat with Ashley in a way that let Ashley feel seen and heard. Beyond any of these great qualities, Janet lived by example, anchored in faith. Her faith came first in every situation which bled into her mentorship with others. Ashley, in some of her hardest moments, couldn't help but be touched by Janet's faith. On the heels of Ashley's postpartum depression, Janet helped carry her through a miscarriage. Leading with her faith, Janet reached her hand to Ashley and walked her through a situation Ashley couldn't get through on her own. Janet simply cared and Ashley admits she doesn't know where she would be today if it weren't for the divine presence of Janet in her life for that exact season.

Years after Ashley's miscarriage, she welcomed a baby boy to their family and life continued to get messy with multiple moves and job changes. At this point, Ashley knew the ropes, but that didn't mean she was numb to the frustration of changing schedules. Her husband had started a new job when the kids were a little older, and his work hours were long, keeping him busy well past dinner each night. Ashley allowed herself to start looking at other military families eating weeknight meals together. Every night she anxiously watched the clock with cranky kids clinging to her legs. She let dinnertime become a major point of frustration in her marriage. It was at this moment Ashley started to wave her white flag to a new friend, Jill. As Ashley expressed how irritating it was to be living with such an unknown evening schedule each night, Jill gave her great advice. Jill told Ashley to lower her expectations, but also set a time for dinner. If her husband was there to eat at that time, great, but if not, that was okay, too. By doing this, Ashley wasn't setting herself up for heartbreak each and every night. She learned how lowering her expectations through changing schedules was key to keeping her family running smoothly.

What a blessing Ashley had with 3 mentors speaking such life and faith into her and her family's story. She had mentors help her through hard and heartbreaking seasons of her life. But she also reached out and asked for help in the seemingly mundane moments of military life. There is power in having the right mentors in your corner. We want and need a military wife community enriched with wise mentorship.

MADE FOR ENCOURAGEMENT

I was listening to the radio the other day and the hosts were talking about a restaurant chain reporting a 900 car streak of pay-it-forwards happening. This made a huge cheesy grin spread across my face. I love those kinds of stories. It made me think about when I was part of one of these cycles. I was pulling through the drive-through to grab a coffee and the lady taking my order told me my bill was taken care of. What an amazing feeling! Right then, I had the opportunity to either pay it forward and bless the next car or stop the cycle. Knowing how good it made me feel and knowing I had the resources to pay for someone else's order, I chose to continue the streak. I didn't want to be the one to break it, I wanted someone else to feel like I did.

Mentorship within the military wife community is much like paying it forward the next time you grab a cup of coffee in a drive-through. Letting the ones who are ahead of you pay your way, and then continuing the streak and helping the ones behind you. I think, as women, we are created to be good at things like this. It's who we are at our core. Author Susan Hunt tells us how "... it does seem that women have been uniquely designed and equipped for the ministry of helper/encourager. Women's nurturing instincts and helper-design do give an edge that perhaps make it easier and more natural." It's in our DNA to encourage other women, and if we take it one step further and become intentional about mentoring others, can you imagine the transformation our military wife community would experience?

If you think about what it takes to nurture, there isn't one big moment. When you nurture a child, you care for them — hold them when they cry, feed them when they're hungry, love them when they feel scared. You nurture in the small moments and over time, big changes can be seen. When you nurture a plant, you care for it — water it daily, give it sunshine, add nutrients to the soil. You nurture in the small moments and over time, big changes can be seen. It's in the small moments, the daily acts of kindness, the small words of encouragement, that the biggest impact is made. Mentorship and helping a wife in need doesn't have to mean donating your kidney. It doesn't have to mean deep, meaningful coffee chats with another wife every Tuesday for 5 years straight. It can look like sending a text to check in. It can look like sending flowers on a random Monday. It can look like smiling when you see her at the Commissary. Mentorship can happen in the small moments.

Maya Angelou says it beautifully, "In order to be a mentor, and an effective one, one must care. You must care. You don't have to know how many square miles are in Idaho, you don't need to know what is the chemical makeup of chemistry, or of blood or water. Know what you know and care about the person, care about what you know and care about the person you're sharing with." When you are learning to encourage others freely, pay attention and listen to the hearts of those you're connecting with. Taking into considering those small moments which make a big difference, you can pursue encouragement without fearing it won't be enough. A simple smile may help lead a newer wife into a place of belonging. Writing a brief note "just because" or taking time to cheer her on can make another wife feel like her place isn't unreachable after all. Making an impact in the lives of others, as a mentor, can most certainly happen in the small moments. You are created to encourage, care for, and nurture. All that's left is to take action and follow through on paying it forward.

BE INVITATIONAL

I heard my husband answer the phone last week in his work voice. I'm sure your husband has one of those, too. There was no 'sir' behind anything he said, so I knew it wasn't anyone higher up in the chain, but it got me wondering who it was because he was more formal than he would be with his buddies at work. The phone call lasted maybe 5 minutes. When he hung up, he told me a younger sailor called to ask if he would be his mentor. My immediate reaction to this exchange was, *wow, that's really cool that someone sees my husband in this light*. Of course, I think he is amazing, but it's awesome to see others respect him like that, too. My second reaction was awe and respect for the young man. What a bold phone call to make!

I'm sure some mentor relationships happen naturally over time, but there are other times when you need to be bold and ask for what you want. Each Navy officer within my husband's community is encouraged to find a mentor. Some men and women listen to this advice and others think they don't need it. There is a Proverb with strong feelings about this particular point, saying, "Those who trust their own insight are foolish, but anyone who walks in wisdom is safe."[18] If you take a look at the dictionary definition of wisdom, you'll find it means "the combination of experience, knowledge, and careful judgment". How can you walk in wisdom (experience) if you are brand new to the situation? If you think I am going to say follow someone who has been down the road before, you're exactly right.

---

[18] Proverbs 28:26 NLT

If you don't have experience, the logical next step would be to get experience. How do you get experience? Well, you can try countless times, mess up, learn from your mistakes, and keep going, or you can find a mentor — someone who has the experience already and is willing to share their wisdom with you. If you go it alone and trust your own insights, you are foolish. If you walk in wisdom, trusting your mentors and keeping great women in your corner, you can find security and safety throughout the challenges of military life. And isn't that a wonderful goal, safety? Oh, to feel safe and at peace as you walk in wisdom. Yes, please! Now, does this mean you will never have hard times? Absolutely not. The position of a mentor in your life is to guide, instruct, care, and support. We still live in a broken world and life will still get messy, but we are promised safety when we walk in wisdom and I don't know any better way than to have a mentor stepping through the dung pile with you.

Research shows that 89% of people who have a mentor will eventually be a mentor to someone else. Can you imagine a world in which military wives are thriving, stepping through military life together with the older women training the younger women, mentors in place, and the cycle continuing? It's beautiful to think about, and this is the whole reason why mentoring is so important. Find a mentor, yes, but then don't break the pay-it-forward cycle.

The phone call my husband received about mentorship was inspiring to me, but it doesn't have to work like that. Yes, those of us wanting and needing guidance absolutely need to be bold and ask for help. But the older, more experienced ones can do more than wait around to be chosen as a mentor. Can you remember a time when you got invited somewhere and felt so loved at the knowledge of being thought of? Invitations are powerful. As a mentor, it is important to remember to be invitational. The more experienced wives within this community can welcome new wives in with a simple invitation. Invite new friends to church. Invite the new family to a day at the zoo with you and your kids. Be invitational and watch women bloom.

Being invitational also means making yourself available. Not every mentorship relationship needs to be heavily structured but consider scheduling regular times to visit in person and talk over the phone. A good mentor sets boundaries, but also makes herself available when needed. Remember, the health of you and your family come first, so it's important to not sacrifice that even when helping another spouse. Regular and honest communication sets the tone that you are serious about growth and committed to the relationship without being a doormat.

A GOOD MENTOR LISTENS

In a family of six it's natural there are times in my daily life when everyone is trying to talk and be heard at the same time. Especially when the triplets, who have very similar thoughts and habits, try to get a point across together. It's madness at the dinner table unless Mike and I put guidelines into practice. I think our routine started when they entered elementary school, but we find it's important to give everyone space to talk, to feel seen and heard at the end of a busy day. We go around the table and share a few things about our day as we are eating together. It doesn't happen every night, but the important thing is it helps their little attention spans learn how to listen well and how to share their experiences. Each person gets to talk and then field questions from the rest of the family. Sometimes the conversation stays surface-level and we laugh while hearing what happened in the school lunch room. Other evenings we get to help one kid with something they are struggling with.

Not unlike our dinner table routine, a good mentor knows how to listen well and speak from their own experience. When you enter into a mentorship role you must always choose listening first. For some, this comes naturally. Others will have to work at it. But in order to create the necessary trust this relationship needs, you must be an expert listener. As the mentor it's important to give the mentee space to vent and talk through their struggles. As the person who has gone before them, you can ask the tough questions in order for them to grow. If you are doing all the talking, they'll never get the help they need.

If my kids are getting antsy or bored while someone else is talking at the dinner table, we encourage them to make eye contact. This might sound obvious, but real eye contact and genuine conversation has taken a backseat in today's society with how focused we are on our phones. Engaging in the conversation or keeping it going by asking open-ended questions is another tool we suggest as the chatter continues around the table. Being a good listener is hard work and as they are eating and busy with their hands, we find it less likely for them to get fidgety. But once their plate is clean, it's harder for them to focus on whoever is sharing. I need this reminder just as much as they do. We find it's helpful to hold our cups in our hands while we are listening. I take this same advice with me into coffee shops when I am meeting with a friend or mentee. Beyond all these great tools, the biggest hurdle we face is interrupting. Becoming a good listener requires us to bite our tongues even when we want to interject.

None of this is groundbreaking information but refreshing and utilizing these skills is helpful throughout a mentor relationship. If part of our goal within the military wife community is to improve its overall wellness, we must learn to care for one another through listening.

CONFIDENT LEADERSHIP

Ever since I've known him, my father-in-law has gone on an annual guided hunt. He grew up hunting deer in central Pennsylvania and can tell stories of his time in the Air Force, stationed in Alaska and hunting moose. He isn't new to this lifestyle and always has a freezer full of meat to feed his family. When he goes on guided hunts now, as an experienced adult, he doesn't show up to an area of woods with only a list of dos and don'ts. Whether he is in the mountains of Montana or the hills of Virginia, he walks with a trusted guide. He follows in the guide's footsteps, looks where he looks, and hopefully brings meat home to fill the freezer yet again. The guide doesn't shoot the gun for him. The guide doesn't carry the load. The guide uses his own expertise to lead until they arrive at the goal together.

Mentorship can be a lot like this sometimes. As a mentor you can do a lot of your leading by example. The mentee will watch what you do in your own life and mimic your actions. As a guide, you can show a person a lot by leading a life that matches what you are encouraging your mentee to do. No one wants to get advice and direction from someone who doesn't practice what they preach. A good leader isn't a problem solver, though. Your role is not to tell her how to live her life. You are not her problem solver, but you are her guide. Doing this well takes confidence. A good mentor isn't prideful, but is confident in what he or she knows. I've heard confidence defined as firm trust or clear-headed. I've heard it defined as feeling certain. Whichever definition you relate to, do you feel like you are a confident woman? It's especially difficult to mentor someone when you are uncertain.

The guides my father-in-law uses are not new to hunting. They gain confidence through experience. Because they're dealing with nature and wild animals, there is always a sense of uncertainty, but the guide is confident within the boundaries of his control. It's no different for us as military wives. We will certainly come across new situations and experiences but being able to look for someone else further along and leaning on their confidence is key.

This doesn't mean you must dedicate your entire time as a military wife to mentoring others and seeing them safely through every situation. Throughout your time alongside your husband in the military, you will be looked to as someone with more experience than someone else. When this happens, you can learn what it looks like to be a confident leader. Confident leadership, just like the hunting guide, is about focusing on the individual, not the issue. It's more than just getting the right answer or knowing the solution. You must remember you are impacting real, live people and pouring into the overall health of our military wife community.

You can do this by offering more questions than statements as you guide others. You can trust your own experiences, even if you are only a few months ahead on your own military wife journey. You can approach each conversation and situation with humility. You can brainstorm ideas together as mentor and mentee. Above all, as you learn to find your place as a military wife and guide others, you can refresh your mindset by saying no to the negative voices in your head and clinging to the truths that you belong, you are purposed for this, and you have a place.

OPEN FOR ACCOUNTABILITY

During one of my husband's deployments, I made it a goal of mine to get in shape. I'll admit the driving force behind this decision had nothing to do with my own wellness, though it was a great added benefit. I wanted to be all kinds of toned and sexy when he saw me again after seven months apart. The problem was I had triplet newborns and a toddler to care for. Those four darling children left my stomach scarred and flabby. I claimed I had no time to eat right or workout. I made excuses before I even started my weight loss journey. I mean, I'll be honest. Triplets and a deployed husband were pretty great excuses for just about anything. I played those cards until the deck was worn out. But if you haven't been able to tell so far, I'm an extremely goal-oriented person, so eventually I had to put the cards away and figure out how to make this dream a reality.

It wasn't until I joined an accountability group that I started making significant progress. I had a personal coach walking me through the basics of healthy eating, portion control, proper weight loss techniques, and safe workout habits. I knew I couldn't make all these changes by myself, but having a mentor, someone further along in her own journey, made all the difference. We had regular meet times and she wasn't afraid to keep me accountable. She knew my specific goals and helped me reach them over the course of the deployment. She also took time to critique my routines, workouts, and eating habits. Trying my hardest to let her lead me, I was forced to swallow my pride and take her constructive criticism.

Besa Pinchotti reminds us that "[we must] normalize talking about hard topics." Part of being a good mentor means not being afraid to have the hard conversations. Of course, we must learn to do this with grace, gentleness, and love, but we can't ignore the hard things. My health coach was truly trying to help me improve in multiple areas of my life. The core of her work and expertise landed within the scope of physical wellness, but if you've ever been down the weight loss road, you know how much of it bleeds into every other area of your life. If I wanted to see progress, I needed to be open, and she needed to be bold enough to look at my situation with a critical eye and provide constructive criticism.

This is no easy task, and there is much more to being a mentor than simply being an accountability partner, but a good mentor has this skillset, too. First, as you learn to critique and hold others accountable, you must set boundaries. It was so tempting for me to have my coach on speed dial, FaceTiming her to check my lunch portions or give me a pep talk before my morning workout. I needed so much training and guidance in those beginning days, but she was firm with her boundaries and commitments to her own family. It in no way negatively impacted my results, but showed me how much balance a healthy lifestyle can bring. Next, you must be encouraged to set realistic goals and stand firm, not letting excuses get in the way. As I met with my coach each week, I would express my dreams and vision for the deployment homecoming — what dress I wanted to wear, how I wanted to feel, what weight I wanted to be. She, with grace and care, helped guide my dreams into realistic goals so that I wouldn't get trapped with unrealistic expectations. She was specific throughout this process and never relied on generalizations.

Throughout the months of deployment, I hit periods of great growth and other times I felt like I was going backwards. Each and every step of the way my coach provided me with actionable recommendations to get through the current phase. Through it all she coached with grace. She was full of kindness in her posture and words because she understood she was mentoring a real person instead of focusing on the assignment. She was able to keep me accountable, pour into my life in a positive way, and mentor me with amazing success. It was one of the most rewarding moments when my husband stepped off the bus and I felt confident and sexy as we hugged and kissed for the first time in seven months. I realized later how my goal of getting fit for homecoming went much deeper. I was craving for my place as a military wife to be solidified. I wanted to be able to stand strong on the day of his return. I wanted and needed to feel like I could make him proud as I stood by his side, united in his mission, with our right community surrounding us, confident in who I was as a military wife. In that season, I wasn't able to find that place without my health coach. It took asking for help and bringing people into my life to help me, and I will never forget how much of a difference that made.

TRUST ONE ANOTHER

Earlier in the chapter we defined mentorship as the influence, guidance, or direction given by a trusted counselor or guide. We used the word "trusted". How many of us have a story of when we confided in a friend only to find out they betrayed our trust and told countless others? How many of us have been on the other side of this? I can remember a time when I was confronted by a close friend after she found out I had gossiped about her. I had betrayed her trust, and the wounds took a long time to heal. Trust is vital in every relationship, including mentorship relationships.

At one point or another in your time as a military wife, you will be reaching out to a new wife. You will help her get unpacked, help watch her kids when the moving truck arrives, help explain an insurance question, or help her understand how to address her husband's boss. The list is long and throughout these interactions a level of trust must be maintained. If at some point you are watching her kids as the moving truck arrives and her four-year-old tells you how Mommy and Daddy were screaming at each other last night, this isn't an invitation for you to text your best friend and spread gossip about how the new family's marriage is on the rocks. If you meet another wife for coffee and she confides in you about her mental health struggles, it is not meant to be broadcasted to anyone else.

When you are in a position of mentorship with another wife, you absolutely cannot betray the trust built within that relationship. If you step into this role, however large or small, you have proven yourself trustworthy and it should remain a safe place for both people. Crossing that line of confidentiality and trust can ruin not only her position within the situation, but your own reputation as well. As you gain trust with those you are mentoring, you must lead by example and be open and honest with them. You can ask for specific needs, but above all you must not gossip to others. Lastly, if you are comfortable with it, pray with and for that person. Prayer is a great way to break down walls and build a new foundation in trust.

When trust is broken it fuels feelings of bitterness, betrayal, anger, and hurt. There are consequences to breaking someone's trust and if you truly care about the health of the military wife community, you will keep this in mind as you guide others through their journey.

COMPASSIONATE HEARTS

Several years ago, I took a spiritual giftings test as part of a church group. There are roughly twenty spiritual gifts, and the test is meant to help you discover your own giftings from God. It wasn't too surprising to see the gift of exhortation (encouragement) ranked in the top as I am one who values encouragement, so therefore like to encourage others. What was surprising, however, was my score for the gift of mercy. On a scale from 0-12, my score for the gift of mercy is a zero. Somewhere deep inside, I knew I wasn't a very compassionate, merciful person, but to see a big fat zero on the paper made it a little more real. Years later when I took the Enneagram test and discovered I was a 3, things started coming together for me. The way I'm wired doesn't always show compassion first, but it doesn't mean I can't work on it.

When I am mentoring someone, I have to work really hard to remember that the woman across the table has feelings just like I do. I have to remember she is going through something she has never experienced before and she doesn't know how to feel or act. This isn't a natural train of thought for me, but it's a weakness I'm willing to work on so that I can pour into the lives of others with mercy and compassion. As a mentor I have to remember what it was like for me when I was in her position. I am good at being a cheerleader and handing out encouragement like candy at a parade, but sometimes it comes across weak and almost fraudulent because it isn't coming from a place of mercy.

For me, this goes hand in hand with passing judgment. I must remember how the woman across the table is most likely already facing judgment from others and she is coming to me as a safe person. As her mentor, I must stay trustworthy and compassionate toward her situation without passing judgment. Just because I am her mentor and more experienced in this one area doesn't mean I am better or more righteous. I am her resource and guide. If you are someone like me, I find it helpful to take lots of deep breaths before and during mentorship conversations.

Once I can trust myself to be fully present with that person, I picture Jesus standing over her shoulder. The woman across from me is His child and everything I say to her must be able to be said in the presence of her Father. It's an amazing image to call to mind — one that is humbling and full of mercy.

We, as military wives, are all doing the best we can with what we know. When you enter into mentorships it's important to lead well without persecution. A good mentor is someone the mentee will likely never forget. They'll remember the dedication, gentleness, mercy, compassion, unwavering support, accountability, and confidence. Let's do our best to mentor with these same qualities.

Battle Buddy: Peyton

Peyton never would have made it up the mountain without Caitlyn. A literal mountain. Mount Lamlam is the highest peak on the island of Guam. According to many hikers the trail can be difficult to follow during certain times of the year when the natural vegetation is overgrown. It's recommended to hike with someone else, preferably someone who has experience on the mountain.

Peyton, a Navy wife, remembers her first few years of military life vividly. Her initial weeks on the island of Guam were extremely lonely. In her own words, she remembers feeling like she was "floating through her early spouse experience". Without much direction or confidence, she stepped out with boldness and started meeting other spouses on the remote island. Caitlyn had been living in Guam for over two years, and when she met Peyton, she simply invited her into her life. Caitlyn started with an invite to church, welcoming Peyton and her husband into a congregation of loving people. Next, Caitlyn invited Peyton to go on a hike with her. As Peyton followed Caitlyn's twisting path up the mountain, she started to realize the importance of having a guide. Without an experienced leader, Peyton wouldn't know to turn right at the tree and go left around the mud pit. Together, with Peyton following Caitlyn, they made it up Mount Lamlam together. Having a guide on her journey was crucial to Peyton's success.

After their shared experience, a bond was formed. Before long, Peyton was going to Caitlyn for all sorts of information about not only military life, but the local community as well. It was because Caitlyn had experience to speak from that she was able to reach out her hand to Peyton and lead her deeper into military wife life. Before finding a friend and mentor to help walk her through military wife life, Peyton admits to feeling isolated. But sometimes the good Lord shines on us in ways we never expect, and Peyton found Caitlyn. Caitlyn continued to help and guide Peyton through those sometimes challenging early military wife years.

Caitlyn and her husband left the island first, but the two women kept in touch and were gifted another set of orders together, in Virginia. Because Caitlyn and Peyton had already established a strong mentor relationship, they fell into step again without hesitation. In Virginia, Caitlyn helped Peyton through her first pregnancy. When Peyton had questions about nursing and pumping, she called Caitlyn. When Peyton was uncertain of her next steps as a military wife, she could trust Caitlyn to volunteer information.

When asking Peyton what qualities she values within her mentorship and friendship with Caitlyn, she highlights being invitational, quick to listen, willing to help, and being in a similar season of life regardless of age. Because of that positive mentor relationship early in her military wife journey, Peyton understands the value of being guided through what can be a difficult situation sometimes.

Now, Peyton doesn't hesitate to invite new faces along on her own journey. After Caitlyn left the island, Peyton started leading other new wives up the mountain. The one guided became the guide and I can't think of a better image of the importance of mentorship within our military wife community.

USE WHAT YOU HAVE

I can remember the first time we tried to use military flights for a trip from coast to coast. We were living in Nevada and our entire family was back on the east coast. We wanted to travel home for the holidays, and I had heard murmurs of a mystical discounted travel system called Space A. I attempted to do my own research, but like most government websites, I found it insanely difficult to find good, up-to-date information about the flights. I spent what felt like hours reading blogs and searching online forums to find out as much as I could about flying Space A. I learned a little bit after all that time spent, but I still had dozens of questions. It wasn't until I found someone who had gone before me that I felt confident enough to make concrete travel plans. I needed an experienced Space A traveler to show me the ropes, tell me the secrets, and walk me through the process so I didn't screw anything up and miss Christmas.

Maybe you're thinking you aren't ready to give advice or take on a mentorship role in someone else's life. Maybe you're thinking there is still so much you have to learn about military life, and you have no clue what you are doing. I feel this too, some days. But let's not over-complicate the definition and role of a mentor. You may be a military wife who has been doing this gig for eighteen years and still know nothing about an OCONUS (Outside the Continental United States) move. You may be a brand-new wife who had her first duty station overseas. You may be a thrifty military wife who knows all the ins and outs of Space A flights and travel discounts. We need you! Don't discount what you know because you are new or young. On the flipside, don't think you know it all because you've been around forever. That's the beauty of our community; we all go through the same things for the most part, but on different timelines. We all need each other. Don't you dare discount your knowledge and experience. Use what you have and what you know to help those who haven't walked your journey yet regardless of their husband's rank or your age.

Do you know what my favorite advice from a mentor was? It's so silly, but it has saved my sanity over the years. Before my husband's first deployment one of my mentors told me to switch to paper plates. I looked at her like she was crazy. I had so many excuses why I wasn't going to do this — it was going to ruin the environment, I'm a strong enough woman to keep up with the dishes while my husband is gone, it's too expensive, on and on. But do you know what? She had walked through more deployments than I had. She knew my sanity was more valuable than the few dollars we would spend on paper plates for 7 months. Years later, I still keep this rhythm. Anytime Mike leaves, I switch to paper plates. It cuts my time at the sink in half and I have more time to invest in things that matter, like mothering, relationships, and rest.

Being a mentor doesn't mean giving deep, theological advice every week. No. It's about doing life with someone who needs what you have. It's about reaching behind you and holding her hand as she walks through something you have already walked through. It's about cultivating a relationship focused on growth, grace, learning, and progress. You don't need to know all the things about all the things before you can mentor someone. You don't need to be an expert in anything in order to love others well. You just need to be open and willing.

In fact, most people don't want to be mentored by someone who has already arrived. They don't want to be mentored by someone who has it all figured out. They want someone who is just a few steps ahead of them. Don't wait to help someone until you are at the end of your journey. Help people along the way. Share what you know before you have it all figured out. If we take a look at the life of Mary, Jesus' mother, we see a beautiful mentorship form while she was pregnant. Pregnancy can be such a confusing time and I can't imagine being impregnated with the child of God, that's a whole different level of scary. But God didn't set Mary up with his son and then peace out to go handle other things. He is always working another angle, and in this story, he gave Mary a mentor throughout her pregnancy. Someone only a little bit ahead of her, but someone she could trust and walk with. Someone she could share her concerns with. He gave her Elizabeth[19], her relative who was already six months pregnant. Both women were new mamas and while Elizabeth was older, I'm sure they both benefited from having each other to lean on.

As military wives we can take this example and reflect it in our own lives. We simply need to use what we have and remember the tools we've learned throughout this chapter.

---

[19] Luke 1:39-56 NLT

VALUE OF MENTORSHIP: REVIEW

When finding a mentor of your own, you can:
- Acknowledge needing guidance
- Look for the ones who have experience
- Ask for help

Older/more experienced military wives can:
- Check yourself
- Ask if you are living a life worth modeling
- Ask if you are supporting and serving your husband well
- Evaluate the community around you
- Ensure you are taking good care of yourself

Younger/new military wives can:
- Open your eyes
- Pay attention to the older, more experienced wives
- Watch how others love and serve their husbands
- Watch how others live military life gracefully
- Implement what you learn
- Ask for help

When learning to encourage others freely, you can:
- Pay attention and listen
- Smile often
- Write notes "just because"
- Praise their works

When needing a mentor, you can:
- Be bold
- Ask a more experienced wife to mentor

Someone with more life experience can:
- Invite someone new to church, FRG (Family Readiness Group) meetings, walks in the neighborhood, etc.
- Leave several days per month available on your calendar for social events
- Call a new spouse to set up a coffee date

When working on listening well, you can:
- Make eye contact
- Ask open ended questions
- Hold a drink in your hands
- Bite your tongue

When learning to be a confident leader, you can:
- Focus on the individual, not the issue
- Offer more questions than statements
- Trust your own experiences
- Approach each situation with humility
- Brainstorm ideas together, as mentor and mentee
- Say no to the negative voices in your head

When learning to critique and hold others accountable, you can:
- Set boundaries
- Help create realistic goals
- Be encouraging but firm
- Be specific and avoid generalizations in your critiques
- Give actionable recommendations
- Be graceful and full of kindness in posture and word

When gaining trust as a mentor, you can:
- Be open and honest
- Pray with and for your mentee
- Ask for specific needs
- Refrain from gossiping

When working on being compassionate, you can:
- Take deep breaths
- Picture Jesus standing over her shoulder

– CHAPTER 6 –
PURPOSED FOR MILITARY WIFE LIFE

"I want to be known and loved just as I am and live out the purpose I was created for right now."
– Meredith McDaniel, *In Want + Plenty*

When Reality Sucks	161
Personal Dreams and Vision	164
Ready to Quit	168
Living with Hope	172
Through the Lens of Love	175
Stay Grateful	178
Repeat After Me: Mantras	180
Replacing Lies with Truth	184
Jacked Priorities	186
Purposed for Military Wife Life: Review	192

In the beginning of this book, I told you we would be covering five building blocks — five core beliefs gathered from statistics, my own experiences, and the stories of other military wives. Each of these five beliefs ring true for every woman wanting to live military wife life well while finding her place with grace. Our foundational block was a united belief in the overall mission — to be fully engaged in our marriages as we support our husbands as service members. The next block was recognizing the need for a healthy support system as we defined our right versus wrong community — finding friends, setting boundaries, and entering our belonging place. The third block was believing how essential our own health and wellness are — standing firm in our identity, knowing our worth and value, cultivating wellness routines, and staying committed to ourselves. If we stopped here, after all the hard work we've put forth, it would be like spending months planning a Disney World vacation only to bail the week before and never reap the reward.

Yes, each and every building block comes with its own amount of unsexy work, but the fifth and final belief allows you to really see the potential beyond the daily grind. Building block five is fully knowing and accepting you are purposed for military wife life, and we approach this with hope. Each and every one of us will experience unforeseen moments of stress and worry. It comes with the unwritten military wife job description. Military life, at times, will look nothing like what you thought it would. You will doubt your role and let guilt creep in as you pursue your place. You will have to remind yourself countless times to adjust your expectations and stand firm as a supportive wife. You will have to weather dark times while you use your building blocks, but if you do all this without hope, you will never fully find and accept your place in his world.

WHEN REALITY SUCKS

I met my husband at Penn State University while he was in Naval Reserve Officers' Training Corps (NROTC). If I'm being honest, the uniform sucked me in. Like many other military couples' stories, our timeline from dating to marriage was quick. A year into dating he proposed, and we were married ten months later. He had dreams of becoming a Navy pilot and after the wedding and graduation, I followed him to Florida to start his flight school training. Life was great! We were newly married and living in a vacation hotspot. Almost every weekend was spent fishing or on the beach. He was working his way through flight school, and I had a job at a local law firm. To fill our social calendar, we had dinner parties and hung out at Blue Angels air shows. I embraced my military wife role and the community it provided by joining a spouse's Bible study and game night club. The dual-income-no-kids military life was glorious.

The picture-perfect military life was short lived. As the months went by, I started to notice some changes in my husband. He would come home from flight school upset, on edge, and generally unhappy. He was supposedly living out his dreams, but he became a shell of his former self. Soon enough I started to realize the man before me was no longer the man I married. He faced a hard truth, that being a pilot might not be his thing. And as if a switch was flipped, everything started to feel hopeless. The plans and dreams we had for our future with him as a Navy pilot started to crumble around us. **The reality of our situation was vastly different from our expectations.**

Just weeks before this realization we found out we were pregnant with our first child. So here we were, about to start a family, and feeling all kinds of unsure about the future. We started asking questions like, would he get out of the Navy? Would he be able to transfer to a different community? If he got out, could either of us find another job with good health insurance before we had our baby? We questioned everything.

In a series of complicated military events, it was soon decided that Mike would stay in the Navy but transfer out of aviation. Because he had a degree in engineering he was needed in a different community. The months it took to come to this decision felt impossible. It stands true to this today that those were some of the only times I've seen my husband completely undone in tears. I was pregnant and scared of being jobless before our first child would even be born. Mike was going through the loss of his childhood hopes and dreams. I was questioning if military life was for us. We were unsure what our future would look like. Our reality was so heavy and uncertain, I didn't believe there was hope for a better military future. Thankfully, there was another plan opening up, another path. God has a much greater sense of vision than we do, and He was pulling us out of one season to enter us into another. He had a plan when we didn't think there was one; a plan filled with hope and brighter days ahead.

The ladies of Women Soaring, a military spouse organization, say, "[military life] may not look like what you think… [but] take responsibility. Take action." If the solution to an uncertain reality is taking action, what does that look like? What action steps can you take? It's so much easier to pick up the phone and use your best friend or mom as your first line of defense, but what would it look like if you chose to pray first? Ask yourself if you could change your habits by asking God first. When you are trapped in a reality that you don't understand, ask God to invade the situation. Ask Him to assist you with decision-making and to comfort you as you endure hard things. If you can't find the words, just say, "Lord, help!"

In no way should you never share your hurts with those around you, especially those within your right community. Absolutely ask those ho have gone before you to help guide you. Utilize your mentors but remember to pray first, seek counsel second. Above all, you must be bold. As hard as it can be sometimes, you must try to not find ways to escape. Military life will shift — hard versus easy times, busy versus slow seasons, solid plans versus uncertainty — but the only way to persevere with hope is to confront issues head on. As you create your action plan, you must look for the good. The pursuit of silver linings and blessings will save you immense pain and frustration. Yes, your current reality may suck and military life may look nothing like what you thought it would, but there is still something to be grateful for.

I look back through my journal entries from that time and see myself working through this mindset shift. It was messy and full of mistakes, but I cried out to God in that season begging Him to lead us well and give us hope where we felt hopeless. I can't say with confidence I utilized these tools in the right order or even exclusively, but what I can say is now that we are on the other side, our troublesome reality then was only preparing us for something better. Through an unpleasant reality we were able to learn how to live with hope, and because of that building block, I soon found my place as a military wife.

PERSONAL DREAMS AND VISION

There are many things I never understood about myself or my tendencies until much later in life. Thankfully we are allowed to learn about ourselves little by little. A mentor once told me that my experiences in life were not unique to me and that they could be used to help encourage others on their own path. On one hand, that was a relief — to know others were with me on this rocky trail. On the other hand, I felt angry that I wasn't special and unique for what I'd been through. I won't pretend to have a perfect mindset, I'm still a work in progress.

It was one thing to walk through a massive military career change with my husband, watching him unfold at the loss of his dream. It is an entirely different and new experience to navigate my own crushed visions and dreams. As military wives we are asked to set aside so much in order to follow our husbands around the world. If you are anything like me, you've had dreams for your own life come and go. I started college pursuing a career as a coroner, then a chemist, then an engineer. Out of college I got a job at a law firm before becoming a stay-at-home mom. In between deployments and transitions I entered the world of health and fitness and coached other ladies in their wellness journeys. Now I find myself feeling the pull to write and encourage military wives. The highlight reel of my meandering dreams looks very neat and clean, maybe even opportunistic as you could say I did the best with what I had in each season. But the cleaned-up summary doesn't show the full image; there is a dark side to every bright story.

I find there to be a common struggle within our military wife community — battling the feelings of living someone else's life. We feel like we live life on the sidelines, watching and waiting as someone else calls the shots. We struggle with feeling like we are simply a fly on the wall in someone else's story, namely our husband's. This is absolutely a lie, and we'll talk more about lies later in this chapter, but believing this lie can leave you hurting and broken, craving identity and worth. Military life will absolutely look different than you imagined, but how do you pursue your own dreams while serving your husband well in a world that feels like it is solely his?

Hitting hard places in your military life over and over again is expected, but the repetition doesn't make it any easier to handle. I spent long hours on the floor of my darkened closet in Virginia gasping for breath as the tears came hard and fast. In Florida, I texted angry unintelligible messages to my best friends because I couldn't find the words to describe my frustrations with military life. I walked out the front door of our Nevada home leaving my husband with our crying daughter because I feared I wasn't cut out for motherhood. I started and stopped several blogs over the years because I convinced myself I wasn't good enough to write. I both embrace military life and resent it in every season, but I never give up.

Many of us go through military wife life feeling conflicted. We want so badly to pursue our own visions and dreams while simultaneously feeling guilty because we know we're needed as a supporter for our military husbands. In his book iMarriage, Andy Stanley says, "The good news is that God doesn't intend for us to abandon our heartfelt hopes and dreams. After all, He is the one who put those desires in us." It's a breath of fresh air to hear we don't have to abandon our personal dreams and visions. Yes, you are purposed for military wife life right now, but what's the deep-down desire of your heart? Is there something more pulling at your chest?

Maybe you've heard it said, "Take delight in the Lord, and he will give you your heart's desires.[20]" I'll be honest and say I never fully believed this verse until recently. As a child, I wanted it to mean if I prayed to get a TV in my bedroom, I would get a TV in my bedroom. But let's not miss the first part. It doesn't say do nothing and the Lord will give you the desires of your heart. It tells you to first take delight and then the Lord will give you the desires of your heart. What does taking delight in the Lord mean in real life? It means taking special care to nurture your relationship with Jesus as your first priority. When you put the Lord first in everything you do, he will certainly give you the desires of your heart, because then and only then will He know you aren't being selfish with your passions. Get in sync with God and as you mature together, He will walk with you in the midst of the desires of your heart. He always follows through on His promises and this is a big one. Trust it.

In the same vein, maybe you've heard, "wherever your treasure is, there the desires of your heart will also be.[21]" If you take delight in the Lord, your priorities start to become His priorities. Whatever you place value on in this life is where the desires of your heart will be focused. In order to understand this more, you must look inward.

What does your calendar say is most important to you?

What does your money say is most important to you?

What do your friends and family say is most important

---

[20] Psalm 37:4 NLT

[21] Matthew 6:21 NLT

to you?

What are you spending the most time doing throughout your days?

What are the motives behind each of these things?

Chances are excellent, if not 100%, that you entered military wife life thinking it would look one way and quickly found it is an entirely different train ride, closer to a train wreck some days. You may find yourself questioning if this life is for you. You may find yourself on the hunt for your purpose, your calling, something to tether yourself to when things often feel so uncertain.

You have desires in your heart. You have hopes and dreams and visions. But sometimes you feel invisible because you have to live a sacrificial life when you marry a military man. You have to say yes to the military before you say yes to yourself. So where does that leave you and your hopes? Does it mean you have to wait until your husband is done in the military before it is your turn? No ma'am. Let me say it again. You have a place as a military wife. You belong here. You can step into your heart's desires while still serving your husband well. Your heart's desires are real and allowed and validated. As you pursue your own personal dreams, be bold enough to ask yourself why it matters. Be honest about the desires of your heart and have conversations with your husband and family about the timing of your ambitions. Courageously step away from your feelings of shame and guilt and step into what the Lord has for you in your next season.

READY TO QUIT

A few years ago, I wanted to redo the entryway in our

Virginia home. I had visions of adding an entryway bench, ripping out the old tile, adding new flooring, painting the walls, and organizing shoes into baskets and coats onto hooks. Thankfully my husband is a woodworker, and before the project was set in motion we sat down together to draw the plans for the bench piece. It had a shelf at the top for baskets to hold hats and gloves. Multiple hooks would hold coats and backpacks. The bench would be the perfect height for us to sit down and pull on our shoes and boots in the morning. Beneath the bench would be a spot for storage so I could stop tripping over combat boots every day. The plans made it look like an HGTV dream come true, but we hadn't even started the real work yet.

In the beginning I felt energized and ready for change. I was hopeful for a fresh new space which would be the answer to our entryway mess. I trusted this would work, and because we made a plan, I felt encouraged we could get it done quickly. I started the demo work the very next day, and let me tell you, smashing floor tiles felt great. I could see progress with every swing of the hammer. My confidence was still high after day one. The next steps over the next couple of weeks included painting the walls and the built-in unit. Picking out new floor tile was exciting and for the time, I remained energized about the whole process.

But you know what happened? What I thought was going to take one weekend turned into a month-long project. I started to lose my enthusiasm. At this point the bench unit was done — painted, stained, and ready to install. The walls were finished. We were so close to installation, but we needed to finish tiling the floor before anything else could move forward. We did one final push and spent several nights in a row tiling the new floor until midnight or later. We were worn out and definitely no longer excited about whatever expectations HGTV unknowingly set in my brain. The thrill of something new turned into something we grumbled about. The temptation was there to take shortcuts to get it over with sooner, rather than doing it well. We just wanted to be done. It was taking too long.

Does this sound familiar? Often when we have dreams and visions, they are exciting in the beginning, but as time goes on the temptation to quit is strong. Rarely does it turn out the way we envisioned, and we tell ourselves we can take shortcuts, we can give up, we can cheat just this once and everything will be fine. Craig Groeschel, pastor and author, says that right before we fail, the enemy (Satan) minimizes the consequences of that failure. It's okay if the entryway isn't done exactly how you planned. It's okay if the floors are plywood for another month. It's okay if you never start that business. It's okay if you don't chase that dream. It's okay if you don't write that book. It's okay if you send that angry text message. But as soon as you fail, as soon as you slip up, the enemy magnifies the consequence and leaves you feeling shameful. He turns "I made a mistake" into "I am a mistake". He attaches your failure to your identity and leaves you without hope.

You may have entered military wife life thinking you could serve your husband well and be a CEO.

And run marathons.

And have seven precious babies filling your home with giggles.

And be a doctor.

And write books.

And pastor a church.

And travel to Africa with a kingdom mindset to share the Good News.

And own your own house.

And work for a non-profit.

And…

But somewhere along the journey, life started to look nothing like what you thought it would, and you let missteps turn into failures. You let the enemy win the narrative in your mind. You let mistakes steal your hope for a better military life. You let normal failures turn into an attack on your identity. And now you believe you aren't cut out for this life.

Yes, I eventually finished my entryway and it is beautiful and everything I ever wanted, but it took late nights of fighting my own desires. It took sacrifice. It took discipline and work. It took daily reminders of what I wanted MOST compared to what I wanted NOW. As much as I wanted it to be instantaneous, the entryway didn't finish itself. The same is true for our minds. Our society today wants the final product without the hard work, and we have to break through that mindset.

Moving through feelings of frustration and doubt into living a hope-filled life will take a transformation in your mind. Your mental awareness must be enlightened so you know the hope of the calling on your life[22]. When you are ready to quit or give up on those dreams, cling to hope.

---

[22] Ephesians 1:18 NLT

Don't be tempted to live without hope. It starts with a transformation in your mind and an unwavering belief you are not here on accident. Today might not look the way you thought, but tomorrow can be different.

LIVING WITH HOPE

Hope is defined as a feeling of expectation or a desire for something certain to happen. There were days during the transition from aviation to engineering when I can honestly say I had no hope at all. I was unsure of our next steps and I had no expectations. But other days there were glimmers of a desire for something greater. I clung to the hope of my husband returning to his former self. I clung to the hope of us being able to start a family within a military community we loved. Maybe you've heard the line, "hope is a strong and trustworthy anchor for our souls."[23] It's true. You can trust the hope you have. I had hope even though it was tiny. My military life looked nothing like what I thought it would, but I clung to a minuscule thread of hope that it could be better. Even as I navigate my own dreams and desires, I'm learning if I have hope I can confidently stand in my purpose. Even in the middle of my painful, uncomfortable, and insecure feelings regarding my own visions and place in his world, I can have hope.

Hope is an interesting concept. Psychologist Shlomo Breznitz conducted one of the first known scientific studies on hope. He set out to determine how hope impacts the brain using four groups of soldiers. Each group was gearing up to do a final 40 km hike, in full gear,

---

[23] Hebrews 6:19 NLT

after a year of advanced training. The four groups were purposefully manipulated before the hike began. Before this final hike, the soldiers' longest hike had been 40 km, and the first group was told the hike would be 40 km. The second group was told 30 km. The third group, 60 km, and the final group was never told a distance.

The initial idea for the study was to see how the soldiers' performance was affected by what they knew ahead of time. But the results clued us in to something far more powerful. The first group to finish was the group who was told the hike would be 40 km. The second group to finish was the group who was told it would be 30 km. The third group to finish was the group who was not told a distance at all. The final group to finish was the group who was told the longest distance, 60 km. In fact, some of the final group did not even finish the hike. Some soldiers in this group psyched themselves out so much they barely made it the first 10 km before dropping out. You may be thinking, *of course the first group finished first.* They were told the most accurate information, and that's what plays into performance. But what is interesting is that after the researchers took blood samples and tested stress hormones post hike, the soldiers' stress hormone levels directly correlated to what they *thought* the length of the hike would be, not what the actual hike ended up being.

Our physical bodies will only put in the amount of effort needed to complete a task without failure, because it's human nature to not want to fail. But what happens when we have hope? What happens when we are not filled with despair? Breznitz says, "If we do not believe we can make it, we will not get the resources we need to make it.

The moment we believe, the gates are opened, and a flood of energy is unleashed. Both hope and despair are self-fulfilling prophecies." The soldiers' bodies in the final group never released enough energy to complete the hike because they believed it to be impossible from the very beginning. They had no hope.

We know our physical bodies can do amazing things when put to the test, but it all starts in our minds. If we believe there is no hope, our bodies will not show up. If we feel we are in despair, we will live in that belief and never make it to the end goal. Where are you living right now? Are you in a state of hope or despair?

There are many times we may lose hope as military wives, but what can we do? The first line of defense should always be prayer. Prayer and time with Jesus are powerful, but are not always our first thought when we feel hopeless. If it helps, write a verse on your bathroom mirror, on a sticky note on your computer, or on a scratch piece of paper on your kitchen counter. Write down a verse full of hope and encouragement, "so we don't look at the troubles we can see now; rather, we fix our gaze on things that cannot be seen. For the things we see now will soon be gone, but the things we cannot see will last forever.[24]" If you want this verse in my words, try this.

It might suck now but it won't suck forever. Have hope.

You don't have to overcomplicate your prayer life. Talk to Jesus like you talk to your bestie. Chat with him when you are washing your hair and let him know your honest thoughts. He's a big God and He can handle anything you

---

[24] 2 Corinthians 4:18 NLT

throw at Him. If you are struggling to believe He can help you in your hopelessness, tell Him! Be honest and then pray through the verse on your mirror. This may not fix everything right away, but it certainly won't make anything worse. The battle begins and ends in your mind.

Lastly, after you give it all to Jesus, don't sit in solitude. God is really good at using other, trusted people to help you navigate through your junk. Be honest with a good friend in your right community and admit you feel hopeless sometimes. Connection is important and powerful in times of despair. Your limited perspective may be holding you back, but when you release it and welcome in the greater perspective of someone on the outside, you give room for hope.

THROUGH THE LENS OF LOVE

I can remember exactly where I was when the idea of being purposed for military wife life connected for me. It was our seventh year of Navy life and we were stationed in Virginia Beach, Virginia. I was on the phone with another Navy wife and was pacing around my dining room. There were tears falling from my jawline onto Play-Doh encrusted carpet beneath my bare feet. The triplets were potty training, I hadn't changed out of my bathrobe in days, and I had showered only twice in two weeks. I know these random facts because I documented every last detail in my journal. My exact words were these:

"WHY DID YOU PUT ME HERE, LORD? The daily grind is getting freaking old and I find almost zero joy in my current situation. I am so jealous of my husband. So unhealthily jealous that

he doesn't have to stay here every day. So jealous of his life. Maybe I should just leave and see how well he can handle it all - maybe I'd be appreciated then. Today, I hate my life. Today, it sucks. Today, I am angry at God for one of the first times I can remember in my life. I sit here and cry trying to figure out my joy and purpose in this terrible world, and I fail 100% of the time. What am I doing?"

I spewed every last ounce of anger and frustration onto those journal pages first thing that morning. Several hours later I found myself still sobbing and made the phone call to a friend, desperate for solidarity. The questions wouldn't stop swirling in my mind. Why was I here? What was my purpose? What was I doing? Can I tell you exactly what was said during the phone call that November day? No, but the message I received was this: You are loved. Over the next several days I felt the weight start to lift and my burdens lessened. As much as I felt invisible and bitter, I held on to one solid truth. There was a God much bigger than my current situation who saw the path ahead, who knew the brokenness in my heart, and still chose to love. He knew this day was coming. He knew I'd feel as if the bottom had fallen out from beneath my fragile world, and yet he still loved.

From that moment on I saw my circumstances through a new lens. If I have a Father in Heaven whom I love, how can I be miserable with what He has given me? If I know He loves me and wants the best for me, then I must be in the right place. It's logical. If you have a parent who loves and cares for you, wouldn't they put you in situations that are best for you? If I fully believe my Creator loves me, then I also have to believe He has me right where I am supposed to be. Only an enemy would put me in a dangerous or tortuous situation.

My new filter through which I viewed all of my surroundings was love. God's love was greater than potty training triplets. God's love was greater than field exercises. God's love was greater than a start-up business. God's love is greater than whatever situation you find yourself in right now. Because He loves us, He will protect us. Because He loves us, He will help us grow in the hard seasons of life. Because He loves us, He will be with us as we serve our husbands well and find our place in this crazy beautiful military life.

Have you been in this moment? Have you been desperate for reassurance, affirmation, and love? Let's take a look at what Jesus has to say. These are the two verses I wrote down a few days after my meltdown. They are still foundational verses for me when I question my place in this military life.

*"God the Father knew you and **chose you** long ago, and his Spirit has made you holy. As a result, you have obeyed him and have been cleansed by the blood of Jesus Christ. May God give you more and more grace and peace."*
1 Peter 1:2 NLT (emphasis added)

*"Even before he made the world, God loved us and **chose us** in Christ to be holy and without fault in his eyes. God decided in advance to adopt us into his own family by bringing us to himself through Jesus Christ. This is what he wanted to do, and it gave him*

*great pleasure. So we praise God for the glorious grace he has poured out on us **who belong** to his dear Son."*
Ephesians 1: 4-6 NLT *(emphasis added)*

Did you catch it? You are *chosen* and you *belong*. It used to be that only the people of Israel could claim this statement. Now, because of Christ, all believers belong to God and are *chosen*. He chose you. He chose exactly you, just the way you are, to be here in this place. He chose you to be a rockstar military spouse who loves and supports her husband well. He chose you to stand in His love because you are purposed for greatness right where you are. You belong here. He chose you for this and you can begin to view your circumstances through a lens of love.

STAY GRATEFUL

In moments of perceived desperation there is one simple way to cultivate a more hopeful outlook. Gratitude. Gratitude helps us find hope. Gratitude brings hope to dark seasons. Posturing our hearts and minds toward thanksgiving allows space for hope to grow. We can all agree it is easier to feel grateful when life is going great. When things are going your way, there are plenty of things to be grateful for.

You got the duty station you wanted? *Woohoo, thank you Jesus!*

Your husband got the promotion he worked so hard for? *Thank you, Jesus!*

When things don't go our way, we have a tendency to whine, complain, and pass the blame.

Out of 21 location choices, you got stationed at your

21st choice? Lord, why did you send us here? Didn't you hear our prayers? This isn't what we wanted!

Your husband got skipped over this year? This isn't fair! Nothing is going our way right now and no one sees how hard he has been working.

It's human nature and a hard trap to avoid, but with the strength of the Holy Spirit living in you, you can choose to be grateful even in the hard seasons. You can choose to thank Jesus even when this life doesn't look like what you thought it was going to. Deep down you may know you are meant to be a military wife, but we all lose hope sometimes. By creating a habit of gratitude, you can stand in your purpose. When you focus on the good things around you, you see more good things. Same goes for the negative. What you focus on expands. What you spend time cultivating grows.

In times of disappointment and frustration, I can promise gratitude will not come naturally. I can promise it will take intentionality to find the good. I can promise your physical body will want to throw a pity party and never find anything to be thankful for. I can also promise you have the strength to be grateful at all times. You have the strength to live military wife life on purpose and for a purpose. I've always admired women who can keep regular gratitude journals. I am not a consistent gratitude journaler, but maybe someday I'll tackle that goal. There are so many great options for gratitude journaling and I challenge both of us to find one that works for us.

One way I intentionally insert gratitude into my daily routine, especially when I'm not doing a good job of keeping my journal, is through my prayer time. Someone a long time ago taught me to start every prayer with what I am thankful for. I vaguely remember this being modeled for us in the Lord's prayer, and after years of practice, it has become a habit of mine to start each prayer with the praises. Often it is tempting to dive into what you want and need, but try listing what you are grateful for first.

Another way I encourage myself to bring gratitude into my daily and weekly routines is by using alarms on my phone. I love setting alarms, not just in the mornings, but for random things throughout my week. For example, I have a reminder on my phone to pray for specific friends throughout the week. Every Friday and Monday my phone chirps at 1:00 p.m. EST to pray for Jess and her family. Using this same method for being more intentional with my gratitude practice means setting a reminder to name what I'm thankful for. I find that I'm least likely to naturally want to do this during the most chaotic times of my day. It's tough for me to stay grateful in my hardest moments, so I challenge myself with a gratitude alarm. If I can practice gratitude in these moments, the rest of my day will feel like the spring sun on my face after a long winter. Regardless of how you insert a more grateful perspective into your day, the important thing to remember is that keeping an appreciative posture will result in a positive mindset shift. Staying grateful for what and who you have around you makes the transition to finding your place a gentler one.

REPEAT AFTER ME: MANTRAS

Throughout the 2020 coronavirus pandemic, my children, like so many, seesawed between in-person school and virtual classrooms. The same was true for my husband at work. This meant for some days, weeks, and months, we were all home. All together. All day. Like for most military families I know, this ended up being more challenging than we realized. Mike's constant presence forced me and the kids to adapt our daily rhythm. We all had to commit to finding a new normal in the midst of a challenging transition. After several weeks of rearranging desks, work areas, and routines to fit everyone's needs with virtual school and tele-work, we seemed to have hit our stride.

Each morning, Mike and I would wake up before the kids, read our Bibles, and workout together. Then it was a tag-team effort to get the kids fed, dressed, and on the bus or to our in-home school room. Once all four (sometimes smiling) faces were out the door or in their virtual classrooms, we made breakfast together. As we were scrambling eggs and toasting bagels, we had a routine of turning on our favorite morning radio show. Bobby Bones has been our favorite for countless years and we both enjoy the culture of the show. Bobby, Amy, Lunchbox, and Eddie have become household names, and our kids love the Morning Corny joke segment. Bobby not only entertains us through his morning radio show, but he is also an author. One of his books has a very memorable subtitle. It's Bobby's mantra — his motto. The book is titled "Fail Until You Don't: Fight Grind Repeat".

Fight. Grind. Repeat.

Throughout the book he talks about how this motto has gotten him through many life situations. Bobby grew up poor and had to continually fight and grind it out over and over again. He is now a successful radio personality, but

"Fight Grind Repeat" has been his motto for a very long time. I don't necessarily agree with 100% of Bobby's methods and strategies, but I do love the idea of having a mantra. Do I think the only way to get ahead in life is to fight and grind day in and day out? No, but it worked for him as he went through life, battling the ups and downs to eventually find his way to his dreams and place in the world.

There is no universal catchall motto for everybody, forever and ever amen. What is important is having something you can cling to when life feels uncertain. Something you can repeat over and over in your head for you to remember the important things, personal to you in your life. You have permission to change your mantra depending on your season of life. You have permission to use someone else's. You have permission to keep one for your entire life. For right now and the last seven years or so, mine sounds like this.

Wake up. Trust Jesus. Be intentional. Repeat.

Waking up before the kids is my sanity, my peace. You've already read about this methodology, so you know I treasure early mornings. The next thing that's important to me is to trust in Jesus. Without the Lord, I know I can do nothing and without trusting in him I know I am a hot mess. Thirdly, something that is extremely important to me, especially as a military wife, is to be intentional. I have to remind myself daily, if not hourly, to be intentional. Be intentional in my marriage. Be intentional as a mother. Be intentional as a writer. Be intentional while keeping up with our home. Be intentional with our finances. Being intentional and stewarding well the things that the Lord has given me is extremely important in my family's dynamic and in my own personal life.

Wake Up. Trust Jesus. Be intentional. Repeat. I even nicknamed mine, so now all I have to say is WuTBiX to be reminded of my mantra. The key is to come up with what's important to you and make it memorable. Create a mantra that comes to mind easily in the hard, uncomfortable, and uncertain moments of military life. Waking up and having a plan for each day will make you better as you continue to do the good things the Lord has told you to do.

So, how do you go about creating a mantra? Start with making a list of the things important to you, including any family values or beliefs. Don't be shy with the list. Write it all down. Add to the list any inspirational mantras or quotes that you love. Remember, it's okay to fall in love with someone else's mantra. If it works for you in this season of life, don't reinvent the wheel. Once you have your list, condense it to two or three items that will inspire and encourage you to not only keep the mantra going in your own life, but motivate you to do better. Next is the fun part. Write your kick-butt mantra everywhere. Bust out the sticky notes and graffiti your whole world. Bathroom mirrors, computer monitors, vehicle dashboards, refrigerators, all the places. Place it anywhere you are so you can be reminded until it becomes second nature to tell yourself your own mantra.

If you're old like me, you may remember a children's book with a very catchy phrase. After the little blue train agreed to pull a larger train up and over a mountain, it only succeeded because it kept repeating, "I think I can. I think I can." Your mantra can be situational like the little blue train or lifelong like Bobby's. The larger picture of both is the same. A mantra is there to help you remember what's important when your focus becomes distracted. Military life will sometimes make you feel out of control and lost within your purpose and place. Having a deep-rooted mantra will help bring your focus back to what matters, back to what is needed to get through the times of uncertainty, and back to finding your place in his world.

REPLACING LIES WITH TRUTH

I read a book in 2018 that semi-rocked my world. I say "semi-rocked" because I think I knew much of it deep down, but could never put a name to it. *Lies Women Believe* by Nancy DeMoss Wolgemuth shined a bright light on the shadowed lies I was telling myself, even though I didn't know they were lies. As a young Christian mom and military wife, I thought I was kicking butt and taking names while also telling myself "If my circumstances were different, I would be different." I loved to trap myself in "if only" scenarios without knowing they weren't true. I read through Nancy's book in shock. How had I been so blind? How was I living so many lies and accepting them as truths? What I couldn't do was beat myself up for the things I didn't know. Shame and guilt have no place in this equation. But I started asking myself how I would discover the lies I was believing, and then once I was able to name them, what next? How could I replace them with truth?

Have you ever used your military life as an excuse for not being able to do something?

Have you ever accepted something about yourself because of your military lifestyle?

I used to swear. A lot. There's nothing earth-shattering about this and no one is going to die because I said bad words, but I accepted it as normal. I thought because my husband's work environment was filled with cuss words, it didn't matter if I swore or not. It wasn't anything I ever felt guilty about. Recently I felt the pull to clean up my mouth. It was no longer a valid excuse, for me personally, to use the military lifestyle as the reason for my language. We are called to love others and I suddenly felt there was a better way to love people than to swear at and with them. Also, I was raising a whole lot of small children and didn't want them repeating my bad language. I had to replace a lie I believed with a truth I could stand on.

Some lies we believe are life altering. Some are small. But as we continue to uncover them, we will find ourselves feeling more hopeful. Swearing or not swearing in the grand picture of life isn't a big deal, and basically everyone around me still swears. My choice to not swear was never about the actual bad words coming out of my mouth, it went deeper than that. My choice to clean up my language was the result of replacing a lie with a truth. It was a mindset shift from,

"My husband is in the Navy and there's a reason the phrase 'cuss like a sailor' exists. The military is part of who I am, therefore I swear too. It's just how this lifestyle is."

to

"It's a lie to think if my circumstances were different, I would be different. I can be a military wife who doesn't swear because I have that choice."

The formula to use as you uncover potential lies you are believing about yourself, your circumstances, and those around you, looks like this. First, identify behaviors in your life that are keeping you from feeling free. Second, acknowledge there is most likely a lie at the root of that behavior. Third, replace the lie with truth. Swearing was the behavior, accepting I had no choice because of my lifestyle was the lie, and telling myself I could be true to myself regardless of my circumstances was how I replaced the lie with truth.

If you aren't sure what lies you are believing right now, I challenge you to pray about it or ask a trusted friend in your right community. If you have the narrative racing through your mind that you aren't good enough, that's a lie. It might manifest itself through imposter syndrome or behaviors like jealousy and comparison. Once you identify the behaviors and acknowledge the lie behind it, you can search for quotes or scriptures that counter the lie. Take your "I'm not good enough" and replace it with "I am a daughter of the King and I am worthy in the Lord's eyes". Then take your new truth statement and write it down in places you'll see it. Give yourself reminders throughout your house. Before long you'll retrain your brain and begin standing on truth. This is yet another tool as you work to shift your mindset toward what matters most, and that's key to standing strong in your place as a military wife.

JACKED PRIORITIES

As tempting as it may be to focus solely on what we want to do and where we are being called, we cannot ignore what is right in front of us. If you were given five cards, one for Faith, Ministry, Children, Husband, and Work, how would you prioritize them in your own life? I think we can all agree faith goes at the top, but things get hazy after that, right? I am tempted to put work first a lot of times. Other times my children hit the top of the list and my husband is lost on the bottom. If we follow what the world tells us, our cards could look any number of ways. Pinterest shames us with organized lunch boxes and perfect birthday parties until we firmly place our Children card at the top of the list. Instagram influencers and multilevel marketing (MLM) mom bosses tell us we need to be making money from our phones, so our Work card comes first. Church may beg us to run the hospitality committee and also serve in the kids' ministry on Sundays, so we place the Ministry card at the top.

However, if we follow the scriptures our cards are ordered like this: Faith, Husband, Children, Work, Ministry. There is nothing more important than your relationship with your savior. Nothing. After that, as military wives, our first and primary calling belongs to our families. Moms, it's a hard pill to swallow, but your husband belongs above the children. The one you entered into a committed covenant with and the ones who share your blood all come first. They are your top priority after your relationship with the Lord. If and only if your relationship with the Lord is good and your family is well served can you give time and attention to your work and secondary ministry.

If your cards are jacked right now, great! You're a perfectly imperfect human. Let's be friends. You will rarely get this correct all day every day, but knowing your priorities is a great launch pad. Yes, the Lord has given you hopes and desires in your heart and He is cheering you on with a chorus of angels behind him, but God doesn't want any of those things to come before Him. He loves you too much to sacrifice your relationship with Him.

When you get your priorities aligned, the great news is He helps with the rest. When you start with Jesus and pour into your family first, the Holy Spirit shows up to help. You are never alone. When you take time to analyze your own priorities, you may find them misaligned from time to time. If this happens, there are several things you can do. First, you can take time to name the desires of your heart. We've already talked about this in previous sections, but it's important to recall them when your priorities are jacked. Second, you can reflect on what gives you passion and feeds into your interests. From here you can rearrange your priorities and cling to hope. Maybe your priorities are jacked right now because your marriage feels impossible, and you'd rather eat slugs than put your husband at the top of your list. I feel this. I understand. As you work to find your place as a military wife, I never promised an easy journey. Think of these cards as your target. It's the goal, and you can use it as a guide to work toward. Even your smallest effort is progress in finding your place.

Battle Buddy: Heather

Summers in Mississippi are miserably warm. Sweat forms in places you didn't know sweat glands existed, and you learn how precious the invention of air conditioning really is. Three days before my husband was to return home from a deployment, the temperature outside reached surface-of-the-sun levels. I had just put three infants and a toddler to bed when I noticed the temperature inside the house rising quickly. Our HVAC unit had decided to raise the white flag. Sigh.

In his book Essentialism, *Greg McKeown says, "The only thing we can expect (with any great certainty) is the unexpected. Therefore, we can either wait for the moment and react to it or we can prepare." He's not wrong. However, I wasn't prepared for the giant pile of inconveniences a broken AC unit would dump into my lap. I went through all the things I knew to do, but eventually came to the conclusion this was beyond my limited HVAC knowledge. It was 8 p.m. and I was living in a rented house. I called the after-hours maintenance line and left an SOS message. Then I did the most logical thing ever: I emailed my husband. What on earth he could do halfway around the world was beyond me, but I needed help and I needed it soon. Because my night was his day, he quickly emailed back and did the only thing he could think to do from a different continent. He messaged the owner of our house, and within a few minutes emailed me again saying he hadn't gotten a response, but would continue to work on contacting someone.*

When I knew there was no instant fix, I started calling all the local friends I had. The only issue with this was that my closest friends had husbands who worked with mine, so almost none of the men were home. But because our military network has long arms and a wide reach, a friend of a friend (with a husband in a different unit) sent her husband over with commercial grade fans to start moving the hot air around. My next step involved a tearful, half hysterical phone call to my best friend, and without pause she was at my door 4 minutes later. She knew at this point in the evening on a normal day I would be preparing the gallon of formula needed for the triplets for the following day, so without asking, she grabbed the Pampered Chef pitcher, measured out a gazillion scoops of formula, and started mixing and portioning out bottles. While I was running extension cords through our home and placing fans throughout, we saw headlights shine through the window. Questioning, my friend ran through the garage to see what was happening. Seconds later she came back exclaiming there was a repairman fixing my HVAC unit! At 9 p.m. and at no cost to me. She asked where he came from, and I shrugged my shoulders as my eyes started to well.

I let the tears fall and thanked God for cool air to keep my babies comfortable and sleeping. To this day, it's still a mystery where that man came from. The property management team never returned my phone call and we never received an invoice. You may laugh, but I still refer to him as the angelic HVAC man.

This was but a small blip in my life's story, but it was an unexpected moment. A moment when I felt terrible for not knowing what to do. A moment when I felt like I was failing as a military wife. A moment when I started to lose hope that this life was for me. I began to question if I could do this over and over as more deployments came our way. I questioned if this life was for me. I questioned my place. I understood military life was going to be nothing like what I thought it was going to be.

And in an instant, my hope was restored by a stranger fixing my AC at 9 p.m. on an August night in Mississippi. In an instant, the Lord let me know that I had a community surrounding me. I wasn't alone on this journey and even when it's hard and looks different than what I thought, I can still have hope of a more fruitful military wife life.

PURPOSED FOR MILITARY WIFE LIFE: REVIEW

When reality sucks, you can:
- Pray
- Consult your *right* community and mentors
- Face the issue head-on
- Look for the good

When pursuing personal dreams and visions, you can:
- Ask yourself why it matters
- Be honest about your heart's desires
- Say no to shame and guilt

When you are ready to quit, you can:
- Cling to hope
- Transform your mind
- Believe you are NOT a mistake

When feeling hopeless, you can:
- Remember "both hope and despair are self-fulfilling prophecies"
- Pray
- Write *true* reminders
- Be honest with a friend

When needing to be reminded of love, you can:
- Read 1 Peter 1:2
- Read Ephesians 1:4-6

When being more intentional with your gratitude practice, you can:
- Keep a gratitude journal
- Start prayers with thanksgiving
- Set a gratitude reminder on your phone

When needing to create a personal mantra, you can:
- Make a list of values and beliefs
- Make a list of inspirational quotes
- Condense the list to 2-3 encouraging lines or words
- Write it everywhere

When replacing lies with truth, you can:
- Read *Lies Women Believe* by Nancy DeMoss
- Ask Jesus and close friends for help
- Write truth statements to counter each lie

When your priorities are jacked, you can:
- Name the desires of your heart
- Reflect on what gives you passion
- Rearrange your priorities
- Cling to hope

– CHAPTER 7 –
BE WHO YOU ARE

"I, for one, get mighty discouraged about finding my belonging place when it takes longer than I want."
— Kristen Strong, *Back Roads to Belonging*

We welcomed our first baby girl into the world on August 4, 2011. Exactly four weeks later we packed a few suitcases, millions of baby supplies, multiple military-issued duffels full of gear, and temporarily moved from Nevada to California for 12 weeks. Mike was scheduled to report to a training school at the beginning of September, and because we had only been living in Nevada for a couple of months at the time, I decided it would be a perfectly great idea to move to a furnished apartment with a newborn for 3 months. While my husband worked and I knew no one. What a great idea.

We look back on that time now and wholeheartedly agree it was the hardest season our marriage has ever endured. He was in a brand-new command with new responsibilities and I was figuring out how to be a mom and do foreign things like transitioning our daughter out of her swaddle. Both of us were in extremely new territories, sleep deprived, and surrounded by strangers. With no church home and living in temporary housing, stress continued to pile up alongside the soaking wet burp cloths and Velcro sleep sacks.

I have two intense memories from our time in California, and neither one brings a smile to my face. If you haven't yet been with your husband during a training season, I'll pray for you now. Our husbands need sleep during these times because they are expected to work with precision throughout their exercises. Having an infant at home makes this particularly difficult. I felt pressured to keep the middle of the night feedings low-key and quiet, which meant I had to let him sleep. Even when I wanted to "accidentally" slam a few dresser drawers when I had to change a blowout diaper at 3 a.m., I couldn't. He needed sleep. Cue my emotional breakdown.

A 3 a.m. feeding pulled me from sleep, and I quickly grabbed our fussing daughter and took her to the living room to feed, change, and do all the things so Mike could keep sleeping. Night after night of this, with little to no reprieve on the weekends, left me beyond exhausted. Our daughter had an especially delightful tradition during this time. Because she was beginning to sleep longer stretches at night, my milk supply was working to adjust, and each nighttime feeding resulted in my milk coming so quickly she would puke after the first two minutes of the feed. Then we would have to start all over with a fresh outfit. It was maddening, and in an attempt to work through my frustration, I grabbed my tablet while my daughter was attached to my breast and hastily tapped out words with tears dripping onto my baby's head.

I angrily wrote two memorable journal entries in that 3-month period. They were letters to my husband expressing my complete frustration and how I would never give him another child. Letters describing my anger in such detail it is hard to go back and read them today. Letters I knew I never wanted to give to him, but that needed to be written in order for me to start healing. We give up so much when we sign on to be a military wife. I hadn't taken the time to grieve these losses, and here I was, emotionally exhausted with a newborn and unsure what life was "supposed to" look like as a new military family.

During our time in California, there were issues under the surface that I never took time to uncover. Our obvious marriage struggles were credited to sleepless nights, but just out of sight was my frustration of our lack of connectedness to the community around us. There were financial issues waiting to be tackled, but neither of us had enough of a functioning brain to have those hard conversations. Mike was focusing all of his effort on this new job, new training, and new position. It was required of him. But while he was working hard toward his dream, I was left feeling like the leader of our home without a clue how to do it. Without realizing it, I was craving his leadership within our home. I needed help. I needed him to take the proverbial reins so I could catch my breath. I had no clue this was my cry until we walked all the way through it and I read my journal entries from the safety of the other side.

I won't share the entirety of either letter with you, but I will share the glimmer of hope. In the midst of rage-filled words there are a few lines of hope, and though I didn't realize it until much later, God was working that time for our good[25].

---

[25] Romans 8:28 NLT

"December 1, 2011
Dear Mike,

I want to scream. I want to run. I want you to stand firm as the leader of our family. I wish you would take the lead and pray. Pray before meals. Pray for our family. Hold my hand and pray with me. This weighs on my heart a lot. I know, I need to pull myself together and work with you, not against you. You are my husband, my best friend! God, help us. We need it. I need my husband back."

We get frustrated when things don't change when we expect them to. Especially when we are in the middle of our darkest days. There may be moments you cry out to Jesus and hand it over to him. You may think your prayers go unanswered when just the opposite is true. Every prayer is heard. Every desperate cry for help falls on listening ears. Every single one. There are almost always moments when the Lord hears your prayers, sees what is best for you and those around you, and answers that prayer in a way in which you weren't expecting.

God heard me on those nights. God read those letters as I was pounding them out on my tablet. He heard them and immediately got to work. I wanted instant results and because I didn't see an immediate change in our relationship that evening at dinner, I thought the Lord never heard or answered my prayers. In fact, it would take seven years for that prayer to be answered. Seven years for the Lord to place the right people in our lives and get us to the right church. Seven years of heavenly orchestration to firmly say my husband is now the absolute leader of our house and I have let go of the tight hold I had on the reins for that transition to take place. Seven years.

As military wives, we will be asked to do things we previously thought impossible. We will be stretched and pulled and crushed and asked to repeat the hard things time and time again. So why do we do it? Maybe lots of reasons, but deep down I believe we do it because we love our husbands and feel we are called, on some level, to be exactly here.

Sure, the suck will chase us. The fear will try to take us down.

We must embrace and understand the mission is not only our husband's but ours as well.

We must find the right people to have in our corner.

We must take good care of ourselves as we live out our dreams and desires.

We must pay it forward to those on our heels.

And we must cling to the hope we have.

Our first two years of marriage were full of hail-Mary prayers and fake-it-till-you-make-it attitudes, so those around us assumed we were kicking military life's butt. Thirteen years into this gig, life looks and feels much different. Just a few months ago the Navy called Mike to tell him he might be selected for a last-minute deployment. This wasn't the first time he was in this position, but our approach was vastly different from the previous times of panic and tears and begging Jesus to let him stay with his family.

When there was a threat of Mike leaving this time around, we changed our prayers. We changed our outlook and said if he must go, let him go, but Lord please let the decision be made sooner rather than later so we weren't stuck in the waiting. It's a new lens. We went from praying selfish prayers to praying for a swift and peaceful decision. We prayed for the right man or woman to be chosen to do the task well. It was as if we zoomed out. Years ago, we prayed according to our will. These days we take six steps back and pray for the bigger picture. It's not about whether or not Mike has to go, it's about the overall mission. When you step into living life through this new lens, you have the freedom to look at decisions and situations differently. Because you are fully submitted to Christ, you are fully submitted to the people making the decisions for your husband's career. You can apply this same mindset to every area of your life. Yes, you need this reminder when the military throws wrenches, but you also need to continue looking through that lens in your own life as a wife.

When a photographer is just starting out, they use what they have. They start with one lens and learn everything they can. When they master those settings, they expand their tools and bring in new lenses. They expand their knowledge. They learn and adapt and grow through their experiences. They become better as they use and learn their new tools. We are no different.

Over time you will evolve. You will transform. You will change the way you approach this life if you are willing to adopt the teachings and building blocks in this book. Sure, you'll screw it up all the time, but the overall goal is to be the best military wife you can be so that your husband can step into his calling without worrying things at home will fall apart when he leaves. He needs you. You will have excruciating moments in your military wife life. You will curse his job. You will hate how you feel. You will regret decisions. You will want to run and hide. You will scream and cry. You will feel defeated. I am not sugar-coating anything. This life is not for the faint of heart, it is for the weak.

Excuse me, what? Did I just say for the weak?

Doesn't every other military guide tell us to be strong? Yes, and they aren't wrong, but they aren't all the way right, either. I'm sure you've heard the phrase "God will only give you as much as you can handle." It's bull. It's the biggest lie you might be believing right now, and there is zero truth behind it. God wants nothing more than a relationship with you. He wants you to turn to Him in everything. He isn't giving you hard things because he knows you can handle them. The world is full of sin and sin makes life hard. The Lord wants you to be able to turn to him in the moments you are feeling weak and vulnerable so you can rely on *His* strength, not your own.

We don't need to be strong. We need to be weak enough to need His strength.

You can't handle military life on your own. You, by yourself, are not strong enough to take on this messed up world. But there is hope. You, equipped with the strength of the Lord, can endure the hard things. Nicki Koziarz, author and speaker with Proverbs 31 ministries says, "... no matter where we start, we don't have to end up there. At any moment of any given day, we have the power to say:

This is changing *now*." You started your military wife journey in one place. The military will move you many times and with each move you will learn more. With each new experience, you will have new tools. You will pick things up along the way in order to get better at your craft. Just because you started in one place, even if it's a place you aren't proud of, you don't have to stay there. You can use a new lens. You can learn more. You can change right now with the tools you've picked up from this book. You can forge ahead knowing your journey is not over. The good news is you are not alone. You have your right community and connections around you to keep at this life. You have a family who needs you. And you have the Lord leading you through.

There's a woman in the Bible who walks through a messy, beautiful transformation, and I can't help but think of her as we close out this book. There are some days I think I am walking through impossible situations, and you may feel this way, too. Naomi's story makes ours look like a light jog through a quiet neighborhood in spring. Naomi's story is found in the book of Ruth. Because her name means "pleasantness" I'd imagine she grew up happy. I'd love to envision her in her youth with a smile on her face. I can imagine her with a sweet voice and all the kindness in the world. I can see her being full of such joy as she got married and raised two boys. I can imagine her squeezing happiness out of life as she watched her boys get married. I'm sure her life wasn't all delightful, because raising boys is full of dirt and broken bones, but I'd love to imagine her handling situations with grace and pleasantness, just as her name describes.

Her story takes a hard turn when after moving to a new city, she finds herself widowed and childless. That's right, all three men in her life died. She lost the loves of her life, so it's no surprise her demeanor changed. The Bible tells us she even changed her name to Mara, which directly translates to "bitterness". She was so overcome with grief the whole of her identity shifted from pleasantness to bitterness. It's hard to blame her, considering her circumstances.

Sure, there are times we are bitter. There are times we walk through hard things and life goes dark for a time. But to go to the extent of changing your name to something that means bitterness? That's a whole other level. It's hard to see the hope in Naomi's story when it looks like she lost hope.

She was stuck in a low place. A place that seemed rather hopeless. I'm sure she was an absolute delight to sit across the dinner table with. I'm sure she communicated in grunts and huffs. If I were her, I'd have taken a lot of my anger out on Jesus and those around me. I mean, how on earth could she continue trusting in the Lord when she committed to changing her name from pleasantness to bitterness? She was owning her new lens and it wasn't a good one. Right up until she says something to her daughter-in-law that tells us all hope wasn't lost after all. In a conversation they were having about a potential new husband for her daughter-in-law, Naomi/Mara says, "May the Lord bless him!"[26]"

Let me ask you, when you are walking around at your

---

[26] Ruth 2:20 NLT

own pity party, do you often find yourself praising Jesus and blessing others? Even in your darkest moments, when you think God is far from you, He is near. Even when you want to stay in the suck because you think it's easier than changing, Jesus is close. He is the transformation we need to go from a place of hopelessness to thriving in freedom. If He can show up in Naomi's life again after so much grief and trauma, He can be here for us, too.

There is a moment of darkness in every good story. Has a friend ever recommended a Netflix series to you, but says you have to make it through the first few episodes before it gets good? Some stories start in the darkness. Some stories leave us wondering if the good parts will ever come. Maybe you are in a dark place right now. Maybe you've already walked through some of your darkest days. Wherever you are on your journey, don't stop stepping yet. The best part of your story lies ahead of you, and yes, that's the most frustrating part of all. It's true for Naomi's story and it's true for your story as well. I guarantee your journey will feel longer than you ever thought. Your dark days, when you are in them, will feel like they last years. But don't quit before the good part! Don't give up on your marriage before it turns around. Don't give up on your family when it's hard. Don't give up on your military wife community. And don't you dare give up on yourself as you find your place.

There are women who need what you have. Right now. The crazy thing is you may never understand the power your experiences hold because it all feels mundane to you. Bishop T.D. Jakes says, "When you are truly gifted, you can't see it because it is your normal."

This military community needs you, exactly you. Our community needs what you have because it's something we are missing. Your unique experiences, if you are willing to share them and use them to speak into the lives of others, will strengthen us. It's part of your place here.

Your friendships need you, exactly you. Your friends don't need you to put on a front when you meet for coffee. They need the real version of you — the one that believes she is purposed for a life of greatness within the military spouse community. It's part of your place here.

Your marriage needs you, exactly you. Your husband needs you as your most honest self. He needs you well. He needs you to be secure in your identity as a daughter of the King. He needs you at your healthiest so he can perform his job well without worrying about the wellness of those he leaves behind. It's part of your place here.

You need you, exactly you. The battle we fight in our minds is exactly that, a battle. You are worth so much more than you give yourself credit for and it's time to step into your potential. It's time to recognize your place in the military world. You are a vital part of the equation, and I am here cheering you on all the way.

I'd love to close us out with a prayer.

Lord, you know my heart beats for the military wife. You know how many years I've prayed for my readers. Lord, my prayer today is that you reveal yourself to her in a way she's never known before. I thank you ahead of time for the transformation beginning in her life. I thank you that I get to be a small part of her story, but I pray for the best parts of her journey to be ahead. I ask that you walk with her, just as you've promised to go before us. You know her worth and how much she is needed within her family and this community. You've known her story since before you said, "Let there be light[27]." You knew she was meant to be in this place, with her people, at this exact moment. I storm heaven with my prayers for her to be confident in who she is as your child. I ask you to hold her tight as she fights for her marriage, finds her right community, stands firm in her identity, mentors others, pursues her calling, and grows in her relationship with you, Father. Hold her close. Bless her family with dedication and unyielding devotion to you and each other. You truly are a good Father and we thank you for loving us so well. In your son's name I pray, Amen.

---

[27] Genesis 1:3 NLT

– ACKNOWLEDGMENTS –

This book was born out of years of stumbling through military life, leaning on countless friends and mentors, and a frustration of limited resources. No book written, whether out of necessity or passion or both, gets to its final form without an entourage of help and support. First and above all, I must thank Jesus and the heart He has given me for our military spouse community. I am truly humbled by His goodness.

Thanks to my family, Mike and our four children, Molly, Colt, Haddie, and Charlie; you five were so patient, encouraging, and supportive as you watched me pound away on my laptop for literal years. Thanks for celebrating with milkshakes along the way. Y'all are my favorite people.

To my editor, Brittany Krysinski; thank you for your patient, gentle, and relentless guidance.

To my cover designer, Andrea Flores; you took my vision and worked a true miracle. Thank you!

To all the military wives who contributed stories and insight within these pages; Monica, Kati, Jessica, Claire, Alison, Kristin, Ashley, Peyton, Jennifer, Kimberly, Grace, Alexia, Alyson, and the ladies of Women Soaring. Thank you for your hearts.

To my hope*writers mastermind coaches, Emily P. Freeman, Gary Moreland, and Brian Dixon; this book wouldn't exist without your faithful mentorship. And to the entire COVID cohort, I'm humbled to know and be championed by each and every one of you.

To my milspouses, thank you for your unwavering

strength. Thank you for being my people. Thank you for all you do for this nation. This book absolutely wouldn't be what it is without you, my readers and fellow military wives.

– SUGGESTED READING –

The 5 Love Languages Military Edition by Gary Chapman and Jocelyn Green

The 5 Second Rule by Mel Robbins

Back Roads to Belonging by Kristen Strong

Essentialism by Greg McKeown

Faith Deployed by Jocelyn Green

Girl Meets Change by Kristen Strong

iMarriage: Transforming Your Expectations (Video Study) by Andy Stanley

In Want + Plenty by Meredith McDaniel

Lies Women Believe by Nancy DeMoss Wolgemuth

The Next Right Thing by Emily P. Freeman

A Woman Who Doesn't Quit by Nicki Koziarz

– ABOUT THE AUTHOR –

Heather Eberhart is an author and active-duty Navy wife who is passionate about helping wives navigate military life with grace, community, purpose, and hope. She currently lives in Gulfport, Mississippi, where only Jesus knows how many moving stickers are on the back of her furniture. Heather and her husband, Mike, have four kids.

You can find her at heatherleberhart.com and on Instagram @heatherleberhart.

– REFERENCES –

(by page number)

Ch. 1: Not an Etiquette Guide

6: Based on my interview with Monica in 2020.

Ch. 2: Belief in the Mission

10: Jocelyn Green, *Faith Deployed: Daily Encouragement for Military Wives*, (Chicago: Moody, 2009), 112.

27: Based on my interview with Kati in 2020.

32: Andy Stanley, *iMarriage Study Guide: Transforming Your Expectations*, (Colorado Springs: Multnomah, 2006), 19.

34: "Resentment," *Merriam-Webster*, 2022, https://www.merriam-webster.com/dictionary/resentment.

41: Emily P. Freeman, "32: Stop Collecting Gurus," *The Next Right Thing Podcast*, https://emilypfreeman.com/podcast/32/.

47: Based on my interview with Jessica in 2020.

Ch. 3: Right vs. Wrong Community

51: Shannan Martin. Foreword. *Back Roads to Belonging: Unexpected Paths to Finding Your Place and Your People*, by

Kristen Strong, (Grand Rapids: Revell, 2019), 10.

51: Based on my interview with Jennifer in 2020.

59: "Our Mission + Impact: The National Military Family Association," video, uploaded November 29, 2021, https://youtu.be/0RKi8h1rUe4.

63: Based on my interview with Claire in 2020.

68: Blue Star Families, *2019 Military Family Lifestyle Survey*, https://bluestarfam.org/wp-content/uploads/2020/03/BSF-2019-Survey-Comprehensive-Report-Digital-rev200305.pdf, 43.

70: Kristen Strong, *Back Roads to Belonging: Unexpected Paths to Finding Your Place and Your People,* (Grand Rapids: Revell, 2019), 26.

73: Based on my interview with Alison in 2020.

73: Based on the National Military Family Association Summit, 2020.

77: Nicky Gumbel, *Bible in One Year App, Alpha International,* July 11, 2020, day 192.

84: Based on my interview with Grace in 2020.

Ch. 4: Identity Matters

88: Based on my interview with Kimberly in 2020.

94: Kristen Strong, *Girl Meets Change: Truths to Carry You Through Life's Transitions,* (Grand Rapids: Revell, 2015), 18.

107: Emily P. Freeman, "169: Create Your 10 Minute Evening Routine," *The Next Right Thing Podcast,* https://emilypfreeman.com/podcast/169/.

109: Blue Star Families, *2020 Military Family Lifestyle Survey,* https://bluestarfam.org/wp-content/uploads/2021/03/BSF_MFLS_CompReport_FULL.pdf, 39.

109: Eric Suni, "Sleep Statistics," May 13, 2022, https://www.sleepfoundation.org/how-sleep-works/sleep-facts-statistics#:~:text=Adults%20between%20and%2064,and%20seven%20days%20per%20week.

112: Based on my interview with Alison in 2020.

115: Emily McDowell & Friends, *A Whole Entire Book of Things I Love About You,* (Culver City: Knock Knock, 2019).

120: Based on my interview with Kristin in 2021.

Ch. 5: Value of Mentorship

125: Russell Brunson, *Expert Secrets: The Underground Playbook to Find Your Message, Build a Tribe, and Change the World...,* (New York: Morgan James, 2017), 7.

125: Based on my interview with Alexia in 2020.

127: "Mentor," *Merriam-Webster,* 2022, https://www.merriam-webster.com/dictionary/mentor.

127: "Mentorship," *Merriam-Webster,* 2022, https://www.merriam-webster.com/dictionary/mentorship.

129: Nicky Gumbel, *Bible in One Year App, Alpha International,* November 24, 2020, day 328.

133: John Maxwell, quoted in *Bible in One Year App, Alpha International,* November 24, 2020, day 328.

134: Based on my interview with Ashley in 2020.

137: Susan Hunt, *Spiritual Mothering: The Titus 2 Model for Women Mentoring Women,* (Wheaton: Crossway, 1992), 146.

139: "Wisdom," *Vocabulary.com,* 2022, https://www.vocabulary.com/dictionary/wisdom.

140: McCarthy Mentoring, "Why Mentoring: What the Stats Say," May 2017, https://mccarthymentoring.com/why-mentoring-what-the-stats-say.

146: Based on the National Military Family Association Summit, 2020.

151: Based on my interview with Peyton in 2021.

151: AllTrails, "Mount Lam Lam Trail," 2022, https://www.alltrails.com/trail/guam/mount-lam-lam-trail?u=i.

Ch. 6: Purposed for Military Wife Life

160: Meredith McDaniel, *In Want + Plenty: Waking Up to God's Provision in a Land of Longing,* (Grand Rapids: Revell, 2020), 23.

163: Based on my interview with Women Soaring in 2020.

166: Andy Stanley, *iMarriage Study Guide: Transforming Your Expectations*, (Colorado Springs: Multnomah, 2006), 8.

170: Craig Groeschel, "Help! I'm Out of Control – Greater Reward Part 1," video, uploaded January 17, 2021, https://youtu.be/5fgRCDHanN8.

172: Shlomo Breznitz and Collins Hemingway, *Maximum Brainpower: Challenging the Brain for Health and Wisdom*, (New York: Ballantine, 2012).

173: Shlomo Breznitz and Collins Hemingway, *Maximum Brainpower: Challenging the Brain for Health and Wisdom*, (New York: Ballantine, 2012), 157.

181: Bobby Bones, *Fail Until You Don't*, (New York: HarperCollins, 2018).

183: Watty Piper, *The Little Engine That Could*, (Platt & Munk, 1930).

184: Nancy Leigh DeMoss, *Lies Women Believe and the Truth That Sets Them Free*, (Chicago: Moody, 2001), 218.

189: Greg McKeown, *Essentialism: The Disciplined Pursuit of Less*, (New York: Currency, 2014), 176.

Ch. 7: Be Who You Are

194: Kristen Strong, *Back Roads to Belonging: Unexpected Paths to Finding Your Place and Your People*, (Grand Rapids: Revell, 2019), 172.

200: Nicki Koziarz, *A Woman Who Doesn't Quit – Bible Study Book: 5 Habits from the Book of Ruth,* (Nashville: LifeWay, 2016), 95.

203: "Crushing: God Turns Pressure Into Power with Bishop T.D. Jakes & Pastor Steven Furtick," video, uploaded April 12, 2019, https://youtu.be/CzP23Zti-YI.